THE CHURCH LADY'S DIARY

Lillian G. Rose

The Church Lady's Diary
Copyright © 2026 Lillian G. Rose
Design and Publishing Support: Global Bookshelves International, LLC
ISBN: 979-8-218-86345-6
Published by: LGR Press

To comment on this book, send an email to the author at lgr9@yahoo.com.

All rights reserved. No part of this publication may be reproduced in any form without prior written permission from the author, except for brief quotations in reviews or scholarly work.

Notice

The stories in this book are inspired by real people and real events. **Some names, identifying details, and circumstances have been changed or combined to protect the privacy of individuals.** Certain elements have been adapted for clarity and narrative flow. The author has made every effort to ensure the accuracy and completeness of the information presented in this book. However, the author cannot be held responsible for the continued currency of the information, any inadvertent errors, or the application of this information to practice. Therefore, the author shall have no liability to any person or entity with regard to claims, loss, or damage caused or alleged to be caused, directly or indirectly, by the use of the information contained herein.

Dedication

To my daughter, who saw me through it all, highly motivated me, and collaborated wherever she could. And also to my son, who has always been very supportive of anything I do.

Table of Contents

Author's Note		1
Preface		3
Chapter 1	Starting Anew	9
Chapter 2	Dora	27
Chapter 3	Gualdemiro	37
Chapter 4	And Then There Were Three	55
Chapter 5	Santos	67
Chapter 6	CLINIC	79
Chapter 7	Saul	93
Chapter 8	Gabriela	111
Chapter 9	Juanita	131
Chapter 10	Tomas	145
Chapter 11	Serious Training and the Fun Begins	159
Chapter 12	2016-2018 Convening in Washington, D.C.	183
Chapter 13	English As a Second Language	199
Chapter 14	The Central Americans	225
Chapter 15	The Appointment at the Prosecutors	245
Chapter 16	The Red Triangle	251
Acknowledgments		267

Author's Note

I never set out to write a book. I set out to listen. What began as a career in international development became a calling to serve—and eventually, a responsibility to speak. Over the years, I've met immigrants whose stories shook me, inspired me, and demanded to be told. This book is my attempt to honor them. It's not just about policy or politics. It's about people. If you find yourself moved, challenged, or changed by these pages, then the stories have done their job. Thank you for reading with an open heart.

Preface

In 1986, at the height of the Salvadoran Civil War, I was hired as a USAID consultant to run a small business development training program for low-income Salvadoran entrepreneurs, teaching them about marketing, record keeping, and writing out a plan that would keep their businesses sustainable. That was one of many projects I participated in during the sixteen years I worked as a technical consultant in different Latin American countries, working for a private company outsourcing to the U.S. Agency for International Development. In the latter part of August of 2001, I returned home after months of working in El Salvador on my last assignment.

I went to church on a Sunday. The celebrant priest was a guest of the church, and he talked about the immigrant population he served in his parish. I was intrigued. I was in the Midwest, in Indiana, to be specific, and as far as I knew, there were no immigrants in this area. I listened carefully, and yes, he was talking about Hispanics. This surprised me.

I thought I knew a great deal about Latin America, and yet, I was unaware of how many Hispanic people had left their countries and were now in the U.S. I waited after mass to talk to the priest. He was curious about me and invited me to his office to visit him. When I went to see the priest, he offered me a job. I told him I would think about it.

What happened afterward is now history. I stayed and began working for the Catholic Church as Deputy Director of the Hispanic Ministry. Work that eventually led me to the formation of the Center that would later help people change their lives as they processed through legal procedures and obtained their legal residence or citizenship.

Throughout this time. we all suffered from good and bad times. Times when the immigrants were persecuted by ICE (Immigration Customs Enforcement), and the immigration laws did not change, and a system that became dysfunctional. Times when there was hope, like the Deferred Action for Childhood Arrivals Program (DACA), which took hold and changed the lives of thousands of young people. Also, the hope in 2007 and again in 2013, when we all thought there would be an Immigration Reform, and it was always shelved by ambitious political men and women who only saw their political interests at heart and cared not for the betterment of their country.

During all that time, I was faced with confronting neighbors and acquaintances who were totally ignorant about immigrants. The final straw was when a friend mentioned that she felt "smothered" by the immigrant problem. I couldn't understand why native-born citizens were unaware of their own ancestral history. It's not "us" versus "them" because there is no such "them." It's all just "us." This attitude infuriated me for the ignorance and, in some measure, racist stance on the subject. When the new administration decided to make immigration the spear of their political campaign in 2024, and then when elected, sought to chase after every living immigrant in the country, I decided it was time people understood who these new immigrants were, where they came from, and what they had suffered to get here. It was important for people to hear their stories, their aspirations, their problems, and their participation in our country, bringing culture, family values, work ethics, and consumerism that improved our economy. Why do I feel this is important? Because we are losing community. We are forgetting our humanity and in the long run, will lose our nation. We need to humanize immigrants and side with them and protect them and not dehumanize them. They do not go out and eat cats and dogs.

We need to understand now, more than ever before, how their stories resemble and are like our ancestors' stories. They, too, fled from unsafe countries. If we were to look at some prominent Americans, let's begin with Joe Biden. Joe Biden's ancestry is English and Irish, the U.S. Genealogists calling him, "the most Irish of all presidents." Bill Clinton, who was born William Jefferson Blythe III, has English and Scottish-Irish ancestry. The Bush family has deep roots in English and German ancestry. Then there are the grandparents of Stephen Miller, the most outspoken anti-immigrant staff member of the White House. Miller is of Eastern European Jewish descent; his grandparents were running away from the pogroms in Belarus because they feared persecution. Then there is Donald J. Trump's grandfather, who left Germany to avoid the draft. Not to mention, Trump's mother came from Scotland; she was running away from poverty at the mere age of 18. Finally, Trump's present wife, the First Lady, Melania, came with a visa from Slovenia (previously known as Yugoslavia).

The native-born are perhaps three or four generations from their ancestors. But they fear that the new immigrants pose a danger to their way of life, potentially changing the "American" culture and, to some measure, threatening security and the economy. Historically, this mindset is known to have led to social conflicts and social change: the American Revolution, the expansion out west, and the Great Depression. Immigrants have come in waves. Firstly, from northern Europe, secondly, from southern Europe, followed by those from Asian countries, such as China. Inscribed on a bronze plaque at the base of The Statue of Liberty in New York Harbor are the words from the sonnet titled, "The New Colossus" by Emma Lazarus in 1883: "Give me your tired, your poor, Your huddled masses yearning to breathe free, The wretched refuse of your teeming shores, Send these, the homeless, tempest-tossed to me, I lift my lamp besides the golden door."

Since the 1940s, there has been a continuous new wave of immigrants, primarily coming from Latin America, that are forming the narrative of diversity. We need to stop telling them to find themselves in *our* story and let us find ourselves in *their* stories and come to the realization that this country is great because it shelters the needy, the disadvantaged, and those looking for a better life. Immigrants continue to arrive at our ports and our land, and slowly have participated in the country's growth and forged the melting pot we are now.

But today, we are living in a very tense time. We have ICE yanking people from the streets and pushing them into vans and taking them to jail cells, even sending them into other countries all without justified reasoning. These could have been our great, great, great grandparents! This is why this memoir is their story; these are their faces, and I am but one voice among their voices.

Chapter 1

STARTING ANEW

The phone shattered the silence at 2 am, slicing through the stillness of the night like a scream. I jolted upright, heart pounding, already sensing something was wrong. As I fumbled for the receiver, a guttural sob clawed its way through the line. The woman's voice was fractured and frantic, like she was trying to speak through pain. "Please," she gasped, "He's going to kill me." The raw terror stripped away any remnants of sleep. I became fully awake, yet moving slowly.

"*Señora* Diana, can you help me?" Her voice shook like a leaf in a storm. "My husband has been beating me. He threw me against the wall and kept punching and kicking me…all because I asked him about a house bill." Her breath hitched, and I could hear her trying to hold herself together. "He screamed that I was a worthless human being. Then he walked into the living room like nothing happened—where his mother sat the entire time, watching, listening. She's just as evil as he is. She didn't lift a finger. I'm an immigrant, you know, and therefore not worthy of her consideration, but she likes the money I make. They want my bank account number and my credit card, and I won't give it to them; they would wipe me clean." Then she renewed her sobbing, "I'm scared they're going to hurt me again. I don't know what to do...I don't know where to go."

"Dora? Where are you?" I asked.

"Home," she whispered. "They are in the next room... talking about me. My husband is still in a rage."

"Dora, call the police."

I heard her gasp sharply, "No, no... he will kill me if I do!"

There was a silence that stretched too long. Then, in a pleading voice barely above a whisper, she said, "Can you come help me?"

I froze, "You want me to come to your house?"

She sobbed harder, "Yes, please. Please. Take me away from here, you are the only one who can help me."

My thoughts scrambled. When I signed on to work at the Hispanic Ministry in Indiana, I never thought I would be involved with a parishioner in harm's way, and I would be driving in the wee hours of the morning to go save her. I knew about Dora's husband, Richard, having a drinking and a drug problem, and her mother-in-law, making her work and forcing her to give her salary to her. It was like Dora was their slave. I had repeatedly told her to leave her home because she was suffering domestic violence. But she was always afraid of what he would do to her and their child. She had come into my office many times crying for help. *I can't just barge into someone's house in the middle of the* night! If they turned around on me, if they called the police, I'd be the one taken away. What to do, what to do?

And then it hit me.

"Dora, listen carefully," I said, steadying my voice. "I need you to do exactly as I say. Quietly get your son, gather your purse, your keys, and anything you need, small, without them noticing. Go to the bathroom and call out. You are sick—then lock the door. Then get outside by the window. I will be waiting nearby in my car. I will drive by the edge of your yard, and you run out and get in the car."

She was silent. I could not see her but envisioned her trembling, shaking with fear and anxiety.

"Can you do that, Dora?"

A shaky breath, "Si…bien… I'll try Señora Diana."

"Text me when you are ready. I'm leaving now."

With that, I jumped out of bed, threw on clothes, grabbed my keys, and prayed she'd move quickly and quietly. The storm outside didn't match the one building in my chest. All of a sudden, there was a booming thunder, the flash of lightning, and I could hear the wind and rain falling precipitously. I started feeling nervous about doing this, but then quickly shook the idea out of my head and hurried on. It wasn't so much the idea of driving to pick her up, it was driving to a neighborhood on the other side of the tracks, poor, out of the beaten path, and in the dark. I hated the dark, but I had to do it to help people like Dora out of that darkness.

No woman should have to escape her home like an escaped prisoner in the night. But that night, if I had anything to do with it, Dora would not be alone. It was a good thing that at middle age, I could still jump up and take quick action. My tennis days were behind me, but I still worked out and was agile enough for this mission.

From my garage, I got in the car and rolled down the windows for an instant, only to gulp in the wind. The wind cleared my head, and I realized how crazy it would be for me to come into their home. This would not go well if the husband and his mother found me meddling. I was angry, having heard news of the abuse, and at that hour of the morning. Finally, I got on the street and sped away. When I was close to the house, I called Dora again. She was crying.

"Dora, are you alright? Is he nearby? Has he hurt you again?"

"No, he is still in the living room with his mother. But I am scared of what they want to do to me. They will hurt me until I give them what they want."

"Dora, I am about a block from your home. Can you pick your son up and leave the house? I will pick you up quickly."

Silence.

"Dora, are you there?"

"Si, Señora, but I am scared."

"Dora, I am going to call the police then."

She started crying and pleading, "No, *Por favor* no ... I will try, ok?"

"Ok, I am coming close to your house. As soon as I see your door open, I will rush in."

My heart was thumping, and my head felt like it was going to explode. *What am I doing? This can go very badly.*

I had entered the neighborhood. There was trash in the yard of one house. Evidently, animals had gotten into it. The streets were not very well lit, but I could make out her small home. The trees all along the way swayed as if trying to reach out to me and strike me. I shuddered. I barely pushed on the gas pedal and eased up to the back of the house. I barely saw her and her son crawling out of the window. Then, Dora and her son ran to the street. I raced up to the yard and opened the front door. The lightning flashed again. As they were racing, it started to rain, and I saw Richard running after them, cursing and showering them with insults. "You bitch, where the hell do you think you are going?" With that, he caught up to Dora and tried to pull her back. The child had already jumped into the front seat.

I yelled at him, "You let her go. I called the police, and they are on their way." I had not.

This caught him off guard, and he released her; with that, she jumped in, soaking wet, cramped with her son in the front seat. I pushed on the accelerator, and we sped off.

I looked through the rearview mirror, saw Richard standing there, still yelling, not just at her, but also at me. I looked sideways at Dora, "*Esta bien?*" (Are you ok?)

Her body trembled as she sobbed and felt the coldness of her soaked clothes…and her fear not for her, but for her son's safety. I tried to reach my hand out to pat her but decided to keep it on the wheel and my eyes on the road ahead.

By the time we arrived at my house, we had been on the road for half an hour, and she and her son had finally quieted down. Little Richie, too frightened to utter a word, remained curled up in silence. The drive had been filled with their muffled sobs, the raw grief of a mother and child echoing through the car. My mind raced—not with words of comfort, but with logistics. How would I set up their room? Make them feel safe, even for just one night? Tomorrow, we'd face reality: finding a son and mother a shelter from the storm of their life, seeking legal advice that could protect them, and navigating the uncertain road ahead.

We reached the house, and the storm, like some bad omen, had subsided. I took them to my guest room. It was downstairs in the basement. I gave her dry clothes to get into and blankets to warm up with and tried to ease her fear and her son's sleepiness. I saw the awful bruise on her eye; it was bloodshot red. I offered her a warm cloth to clean off some blood from her mouth. Her clothes were disheveled, her hair wild and uncombed. I could see other bruises, but mostly in addition to her emotional distress; I empathized with her fear and her sense of impotence.

"Do I need to take you to the hospital? Do you hurt inside your body? Your ribs?"

She shook her head and wiped out her mouth. "No, estoy bien." (No, I am ok.) And she trembled.

I hugged her and softly said, "You are safe here. He is not going to come here. Rest now, we will talk tomorrow." With that, I left Dora and her son in the room and went back to my bedroom, put out the light, and climbed back into bed. As I tried to fall asleep, I slowly remembered how my work at the church had started. How I had gotten to be known as The Church Lady. My dreamy thoughts took me back to that Sunday I had gone to church after arriving from El Salvador.

***

I was back in the United States after a year's consultancy in El Salvador. I began my work as an international technical advisor in 1986. I would get hired for years at a time or months and would come home for weeks of rest or sometimes months to wait for a new assignment. But this time, it was 2001, and I was home waiting for a new consultancy. I had gone to church the Sunday after I had arrived from my overseas trip. The church was an old, beautiful Gothic structure, with columns inside and paintings reminiscent of the Italian paintings of scriptural material. At the altar, there was an eye in a triangle, the Alpha staring at the crowd, and at the side stood a statue of the Virgin Mary and that of Joseph. Listening to the choir, I had sat in church, taking it all in and feeling the beauty of my surroundings. The celebrant priest was a guest of the church, and he talked about the immigrant population he serviced in his parish. He was a white man, about 40 years old, youthful, and very fit. My mind wandered. *He must work out.*

I was intrigued. I had moved back to the Midwest, in Indiana, to be specific, and as far as I knew (as of the year 2001), there were no immigrants in this area. I listened carefully, and yes, he was talking about Hispanics. This surprised me.

After church, I approached the priest and asked him about the people he spoke about.

"Father, I thought I knew a great deal about Hispanics, but somehow, I have missed how so many are now in the U.S."

He looked at me quizzically. "Where have you been? What do you do?" He asked me.

"Well," I replied. "I just returned from a year's contract in El Salvador. I was working for a small private company that contracts with the Agency for International Development."

"Really? What kind of contracts?" I could tell that he seemed interested in my work.

"I was consulting on developing an educational program and teaching its government leaders about democracy."

We talked a little more, but people were getting restless since they wanted to approach him as well. He smiled, extended his hand, and said, "Why don't you come visit me, and we can talk?"

At first, my reaction was to disregard the remark and go on my merry way. I went home and visited with my family, waiting to see what the next assignment from D.C. would bring. But in the back of my mind, there was the idea of doing volunteer hours while I waited for a new consultancy.

A week had passed, and without waiting longer, I decided to see the priest. I really had no idea what I was getting myself into. I turned into the parking lot of the old school named Our Lady of Annunciation. I walked into the office and asked where Father Paul Sawyer's office was. They pointed me to the end of the hallway. When I eked in the door, Father Paul was sitting across from a large table, his back towards the window, with his computer in front of him, and he was typing away. He heard me. He stopped and looked up. He was a tall man, six feet tall, not a towering figure, but there was a certain strength and confidence to his manner that made me feel comfortable. I was starting to feel a bit charmed by him. He welcomed me to a chair, and I sat down.

"Good to see you again. Glad you decided to come talk to me."

"Yes, I wanted to talk to you about volunteering."

He smiled. "Let me begin by telling you a little about myself and our church's needs. Then I want to find out about you."

There was no reaction from me, so he continued. "I am originally from here, Indiana, but in my earlier years, I was up in Minnesota and ran into a Latin American congregation and realized I needed to learn Spanish."

"So did the church send you to Costa Rica?" I laughed.

"Oh no, they sent me to El Salvador. It was a failure or a success entirely in fulfilling that proposition." With a twinkle in his eye, he added, "I succeeded."

Then he looked straight at me, "Do you speak Spanish?"

"I do," I replied, further explaining, "I was born in Mexico of an American mother and therefore am a U.S. citizen from birth. Rather than get a typical birth certificate, the U.S. Embassy issues the family a Certificate called Consular Birth Abroad."

He looked at me, and his blue eyes shone. "So, you are bilingual and have knowledge of the Hispanic community. You are exactly what we need!"

With that, he laughed and hit his knee as if he had found a treasure of some kind. I was surprised since I had not come seeking a job. All I wanted was a volunteer position while I waited for my other job to come alive. It amused me to see his eagerness.

"Father, I really want to come and volunteer for a few hours a week. I really do not have time to take a full-time job; I already have a job."

He looked at me and quizzically asked me, "Really? I thought you were waiting for another consultancy."

I felt trapped. "Well, yes, I am waiting in the interim before I get a call to action, to do some volunteering."

But he proposed something different. He explained he had just received a grant, so he had a little money.

"Diana, I want you to come work with me. Help me do community outreach."

I was surprised! This was not what I had expected. Never in a hundred years had I ever contemplated working as an employee, especially in a church! I was not one to wear my religion on my sleeve. I had gone to a secular private school from kindergarten through 12th grade. I never even went to a Catholic school like my cousins had. Then I attended a small college in Missouri that was not aligned with any religion and enabled us to search our own. It wasn't after I was in El Salvador as director of a teacher's group that the women instilled in me a rekindling of my Catholic faith.

They impacted my life with the stories of their suffering during the civil war and their faith that had gotten them through it.

I was a free agent, used to coming and going, not answering to anybody but my immediate supervisor in whatever project I was doing at the time. The priest was talking about working from 9am to 5pm. I thought to myself, this was having a schedule to come and go, with limited time off, and probably truly little vacation time.

He stood up and waved his arms wide, "This is our office. As you can see, it is a refurbished closet. My desk." He laughed. "This table..." He had corrected his sentence structure..."is against this window. And you can sit across from me at the other end."

Father Paul was obviously pleased with himself, making do with whatever the church had given him to work with at the time. I was later to learn that as a Franciscan, he had taken his vows of helping the impoverished. This would be the purveyor of the few disagreements that he and I would have in the future.

When I bid him farewell that afternoon, I had no intention of returning. I earned a good salary, and I had not asked. I figured what he had to offer would not be much, but that was fine with me.

Still, I replied, "Let me think about it. I will call you." With that, we shook hands, and I left his office. I quickly discarded the job offer and went home to wait for another call from Washington, D.C.

As soon as I got home that night, both my adult children were waiting for me. My daughter, Olivia, approached me,

"Mom, you got a letter from Washington." My heart leaped. *Oh my gosh, so soon? They were calling me back so soon.* I took the letter from her, and both she and my son stared at me, worried. I quickly tore the envelope open and read before yelling, "Yes!! I am on assignment!"

"To where?" My son, James, asked.

"To Eritrea."

"Eritrea, next to Egypt?" They both spoke out.

"Yep, that is the place. Jane wants me to open the office there. Our government has made an agreement with them, and there is a need for a new AID office to run a Women's Educational Program."

Olivia stepped forward again with her voice sharp with urgency. "Mom, this isn't just another field office. It's not like Nicaragua or Peru. This is *Eritrea*. Do you even know what that means?"

"I know enough to trust Jane's judgment and my own instincts," I said firmly, folding the letter back into its envelope.

"Instincts? Mom, you've always had incredible instincts—for *other people*, for helping the poor, the displaced, the desperate. But this—this is different. It's *you* I'm worried about. You. For once, can you stop running into danger like you're invincible?"

"Running into danger?" I repeated, bristling. "This is my work. This is my calling."

James threw his hands up in the air. "Your calling could get you killed, Mom! You're a Latina, a woman of color, going into a post-war country where freedoms are fragile—

especially for women! This isn't just about work anymore. It's about survival."

"She's not listening," Olivia muttered, pacing the floor. "Mom, did you even *research* Eritrea? You're going into a region recovering from war, with a government that's not exactly known for transparency or stability."

"It's a Women's Educational Program," I replied, my tone growing sharper. "That's the whole point—education *changes* societies."

"But you're not going to be protected by good intentions!" James snapped. "This isn't Washington. There are no safe zones. No exit plans. You're walking into a place where being a strong, independent woman makes you a *target*, not a hero."

Olivia sat down on the edge of the couch. Her voice breaking, she said, "You've been fearless for so long, and we've always supported you. We *admire* you, Mom. But you're not thirty anymore. You've already fought so many battles. When do *you* get to rest? When do you stop proving your worth to the world?"

That one landed.

I swallowed hard. "I'm not proving anything," I whispered. "I just want to make a difference. I want to *be* useful."

"But what about *us*?" James asked, quieter now. "You're still our mom. We still need you alive, not halfway across the world dodging militias and navigating foreign bureaucracy."

Silence filled the room like thick fog.

Then Olivia said softly, "Please consider the priest's offer. Stay. Help from here. Heal the women in your own community. There are plenty of us who need you."

I looked down at the letter in my hand, my fingers trembling slightly.

My children—my grown, intelligent, passionate children—were pleading not as critics, but as people who loved me deeply. They weren't trying to control me. They were scared. And maybe... maybe I was a little scared too. My daughter, Olivia, was married and had two children. She lived a few blocks away with her husband. My son, James, was home for now, but soon on his way to a new job in Costa Rica.

I sat down, my mind racing between courage and concern, between a calling and making connections.

"I'll go to Washington," I said finally. "Just to talk. But I make no promises."

Their sighs of relief were audible, but I could still feel the tension hanging in the air.

Eritrea was calling me. But so was my home. And the decision, for the first time in my life, wasn't so clear.

After they left, Olivia went back to her own home, and James went up to his room. I was upset with the disagreement and their stance. I was also overwhelmed by my feelings about the possibilities of this new job and the excitement of the other one. I felt I could not burn my bridges with Father Paul, but I needed to talk to Jane, my boss at USAID, and explore the new assignment before I accepted or rejected it.

Starting Anew

The following day, Jane called; the whole question was moot now. The energy had shifted quickly, and it appeared our government and Eritrea's inhabitants could not agree on the stipulations of the contract, so the project was cancelled. I was truly disappointed. I had really wanted to start the women's education project, which would have been the first in the area.

"Well," said Jane Middleton, "do not worry, something will come up. Things are a bit slow with Latin America right now. Senator Helms has not helped the matter."

"I know," I replied, miffed.

"We are working on another project. They do not want to cover the costs of consultant trips, per diems, travel expenses, and such. They are talking about doing consulting in a teleconferencing form."

"What?" I could not believe what she was saying. What were they thinking?

"Look, Diana, it is just talk. I will get back to you."

"Ok, Jane, stay well."

In a way, although disappointed, I was relieved. No more arguments with my family, and they would be happy to know that I was going to work with the church instead of gallivanting around the world, potentially encountering dangers, which is the kind of adventure I really enjoyed. *Until the next assignment came.* That was going to be my proposition to Father Paul.

That night, I had decided to start writing a journal about this new experience. If I decided to take this job with the church, which I was not sure I wanted to accept, it was going to be like something I had never done before. I began writing:

I promised Father Paul I would stay on for a few months until a new job showed up with USAID. So far, nothing has happened on that front, and this community is growing by the minute. Well, I was hooked by the thought of working with immigrants from Latin America, but I had no idea there would be so many and with so many different problems.

I thought I knew a great deal about Latin America, and yet, I was unaware of how many Hispanic people had left their countries and were now in the U.S. I like working with Father Paul; he is a very humble and kind man, but also very strong, emotionally. I like his strength. I have a feeling that we will work well together because we both care for the people. There is no high and mighty or an ego to worry about. He is down to business and has no time for gossip or unfounded stories. I know I will learn a great deal from him.

***

Starting the journal had been a clever idea. With it, I would record the experiences like I had never done before. Aware and conscious that I had a scared woman and a scared child in my basement, it brought me back to my most current predicament. I did not want an angry husband to walk in with a rifle and blow me or us away any minute. I was very much aware of the danger I had placed all of us in and needed to find a better solution for all involved.

How do I explain to Father Paul what had happened and why I had not called the police? Oh boy! Slowly, the hour of dawn and my tiredness finally took hold of me, and I started to feel sleepy. As I finally gave in to my sleepy fog, I prayed, "Lord, you got me into this mess, please help me get out of it."

Chapter 2

DORA

"Good morning!" He was joyful. Something I was going to learn about Father Paul was how positive he was about everything. Not in a sappy way, but just positive, knowing something good was going to happen, no matter how dark the day. And that was good since we did not know if we would have a few or many dark days ahead.

"So, how do you feel today?" He looked at me directly, with a glint in his eyes. "Ready to take on the challenge of doing a community outreach with mostly men?"

"Father, if today is the day to implement this plan, it is not good." And I proceeded to tell him what had happened the night before.

I was troubled and quickly explained how I had known Dora and her phone call the night before. "Father, I know I shouldn't have gotten to her home and taken them in, but they were in danger, and I was afraid of what was going to happen to her if her husband came back into their room."

His smile disappeared, and he looked at me sternly. "You shouldn't have done it." He reached for the phone. "Are they still at your home?"

"Yes, father, I saw to it that they had breakfast and told Dora not to open the door for anyone. At noon, I will take her to a shelter."

"My concern, Diana, is that this man could come to your home and do you all harm. Men, in this type of situation, are not thinking clearly and only want to hurt and seek vengeance."

With that, he dialed the phone, "First, we are calling the police." Then he pointed me to the computer and said, "Find shelter for them. The sooner they leave your home, the better."

With that, I went over to the other side of the table and sat down, opened my computer, and began searching for a women's shelter. I found one in another city, not far away. It was the Women and Child Shelter of Louisville.

The phone rang, and a young woman answered. "Hello, Louisville's Women and Child shelter, may I help you?"

"Yes," I answered. "My name is Diana Palafox, I work at the Hispanic Ministry of the Covington Deanery, and I have a young woman and child sheltering at my home for fear of further domestic violence."

"As it is," she replied, not making any comments, "we just obtained a space for another family, so we can take this lady and her child into shelter. "

"Oh great!" I was so excited, finally a safe space. "Could you pick them up or do I have to drive them down?"

"Oh no," she answered, "We will pick them up. What is your address? But could you be there to greet us?"

"Of course!" Naturally, I wanted to be there and see them safe. I went ahead and gave her my home address. Then I turned to Father Paul. "Got her and her son a shelter. They will come pick them up at noon."

Father Paul seemed relieved. "Thank God. And I just finished speaking with Chief Pelter; he will send out a unit to arrest this man. He has a rap sheet and has charges for drug distribution."

"Oh wow. I felt the man was evil, but I had no idea of his criminal record, and she would not say anything against him." I continued as I assembled my purse and got ready to leave. "From what I understand, Father, abused women do not say much about their abuser. It is sad and sometimes, terrifying."

"Yes, indeed," he acknowledged. Then, his blue eyes just looked at me intently. "You obviously care about people. That is good. But if you are going to work here, you must learn how to distance yourself from the community problems; don't let it become personal. Otherwise, you will not have a life."

With that, I turned around and said, "Yes, Father, I will come back after lunch. I will see to it that Dora and her child are taken to a safe place."

"See you then." He waved.

When I returned home, I found Dora very anxious, and her child was crying. Her husband, Richard, had been calling her and asking where she was and threatening her.

"Dora, I must tell you. Father Paul called the police, and they will arrest your husband for battery and abuse and put him in jail."

Before I finished, she started crying and shaking. "He will kill me and then take my son and make him work." I could not ask her why she had gotten together with this type of man, but it upset me that women in her situation would fall into the wiles of men like him.

"Look." I tried to calm her down. "The woman who will shelter you will appear in court with you and tell the judge what he has done. He will spend time in jail because he has other problems with the law that have to do with drugs and other criminality."

She was quiet, "But when he comes out, he will look for me and hunt me down." She took her boy's hand, "I am not afraid for me, but for him. He is his son, and my husband does not believe it and treats him badly. So does his mother. They are both evil." With that, she lowered her face and hugged her son.

"Dora," I replied softly, "I will see that you are safe, and nothing happens to you. Somehow, I feel you and your son will be alright."

The doorbell rang, I walked up to the door, and opened it. There stood a young blonde woman with a notebook in her hands. "Mrs. Palafox?"

"Yes, that's me," I said, and I turned to Dora. "And this is Dora Gomez and her son."

"Nice to meet you," the young woman said as she extended her hand, and Dora shook it. "Ok, come with me."

"Excuse me, but do you speak Spanish?"

"Oh, sorry, no, but once we are in the shelter, we have Spanish-speaking colleagues to help us translate."

I turned to inform Dora of this and that I would stay in touch. With that, I hugged her and her son, and she walked into the waiting van.

I realized that I did not identify who Dora and her son were going with. "You are Lindsay?" I asked.

"Yes, I am the one who answered the phone when you called. We will stay in communication."

"Thanks," and I waved goodbye to them.

After seeing them leave, I picked up my purse and returned to the church office. Father Paul was waiting.

"How did it go?" He looked concerned.

I smiled, "It went well. The woman from the shelter was very nice and personable. You know that these people have great experience with these situations. It is truly a shame how often these take place."

Father Paul shook his head in agreement, "Yes, and it is never easy. Trying to help battered women is never easy. But fortunately, we will not have many cases like that."

"So...." He looked at me intently. "Are you ready to figure out an outreach community plan?"

"Oh, I am excited," I answered. "I am going to work with a wide variety of people from all over Latin America, and that is great! The fact that most of that population and at this church are men does not scare me; I am familiar with Latin American men. In my experience for the past 16 years as a consultant, I have met nice men from the countryside and awful, arrogant men from the cities. "So, where do I begin?"

Father Paul looked up at me in a matter-of-fact way. "Just have a seat and make a plan on how to do an outreach of the community, and we will discuss it." With that, he turned back to his computer and left me sitting there pondering how to begin.

Used to being out on the field and not at a desk, I was a bit lost. I opened my computer and began to invoke all the powers of heaven to come and enlighten me. I knew I had to look busy and have ideas, so I started writing.

By 4 pm that afternoon, I had a schedule, handed it to him, and told him I would see him in a couple of days. He was a little surprised. "You are not coming in every day?"

I looked at him as surprised as he had seemed. "Sure, from time to time, but I need to go out and meet the community in their habitat. I need to acquaint myself with them and their situation, whatever it may be."

He looked a little annoyed. "I thought you would design some sort of questionnaire and pass it out at church, and then, we would tally results and see what their needs are."

I thought to myself, *He obviously did not learn that most Hispanics coming from humble backgrounds and far-off places are not used to answering questionnaires.* I smiled and explained what I had just thought. I needed to go to their homes or their workplaces and meet them, chat with them, and find out their needs. Filling out questionnaires was not going to cut it.

Reluctantly, he acknowledged my point and gave me permission to do so. I realized at once that this was going to be a partnership we would both have to get used to. I was going to get used to asking for permission to go places, and he was going to get used to my freedom of coming and going.

With that, I gathered my belongings and left our office. I walked down to the parking lot, thinking about how to see to it that Dora was free of her husband and find a new life for herself. A lot easier said than done.

As soon as I reached home, I called Lindsay.

"Hi, Lindsay, this is Diana Palafox. I was calling to see how Dora and her son are doing."

"Yes, hi," Lindsay answered. She paused. "They are not doing too well. She seems scared and will not say much to our counselors. She is afraid of her husband and what he can do to her and the child."

I frowned. "Is there anything I could do?"

"I don't know, Diana," she answered, somewhat troubled. "It is usually common for women to be afraid of their abuser, but she is a bit different. I feel there is more to her than she is letting us know."

"Could it be that she does not have a legal status in the country?" I interjected.

"Oh, that's it," Lindsay cried out, excitedly. "What can we do to help her? Do you know?"

I shook my head, "No, I am not an immigration lawyer, I have no idea." We were both silent for a minute, then Lindsay remarked. "We have some legal advocates at our organization. I will touch base with them and see how we can help her. "

I felt somewhat relieved, "Oh, that's great! If she could get the help of a lawyer to see about her legal status, and then be able to put that man in jail and out of her reach. Let me know if there is anything I can do, and keep me informed, please."

"Sure, happy to," she replied. With that, we both hung up.

After our conversation, I sat in quiet reflection, wrestling with the weight of the situation and the helplessness that threatened to consume me. I had no way of knowing then that my involvement in the Hispanic community through my church would soon become the foundation of a greater calling—one that would lead me to advocate for countless women and men trapped in cycles of abuse. I had not suffered this type of abuse, but once my husband, during our heated argument, raised his hand to strike me, and my hand stopped him in midair, and I said, "Don't." With that, he turned in rage and walked out of the house. Days later, he filed for divorce. Our married life of 22 years had its ups and downs. I was not bitter, just disappointed that my marriage had not worked out, and I felt betrayed that our vows had not been strong enough to weather the storms. I used to rationalize that I belonged to the generation of the 1960s where almost everyone divorced. But my heart always went out to battered women.

I was blind to the broader struggles of immigrants, unaware of the obstacles faced by newcomers to our county and state. But soon, their stories would intertwine with mine, drawing me into their fight, their fears, and the unrelenting realities of their journeys.

Many were undocumented, seeking refuge from persecution or fleeing political turmoil, simply striving for a better life. I had no idea then how my years abroad had quietly prepared me for the journey ahead.

This last thought brought me back to the present. I walked to my desk, opened my computer, and wrote in my diary:

I hope that my desire to do good will not, in some way, hurt Dora. But time will tell. So much of my work abroad now feels strangely distant. We designed and implemented projects meant to serve the people, yet I rarely had direct contact with them—except in moments that stood out: teachers' programs, mayors' initiatives, and the dedicated staff we worked alongside.

Now, stepping into this new role within the church, I will meet the townspeople—the 'real people'—not just directors, ministers, or dignitaries. Tomorrow marks the beginning of a grand adventure, my first steps into community outreach. I hope to listen, to understand their needs, and to truly connect. It will be an entirely new experience.

I couldn't help but smile as I closed my diary. Yes, a new experience indeed. Not in a war zone, not shadowed by the fear of terrorists in town, not jolted by the sudden tremors of an earthquake like the one that forced me to flee El Salvador. Just peaceful. Calm. And hopefully, not too predictable.

Chapter 3

GUALDEMIRO

My first outing was a bit unnerving. I was not used to canvassing, yet it felt like I was doing just that since I had come to a neighborhood where most of the members of our congregation seemed to live. The streets were lined with trees, their lush green foliage was lingering in August, not yet ready to wither and die--- it was beautiful. It was also hot, so I hurried up the steps to an apartment door and I knocked. When no one answered, I knocked again. After a brief pause, the door opened very slightly, and I could see someone standing there, looking at me.

"*Sí. ¿qué quiere?*" (Yes, what do you want?) I told him I wanted to come in and talk to him about the church and that Father Paul had sent me.

As soon as the priest's name was mentioned, there was an element of trust. He opened the door wider, and there stood before me a short, stocky, and paunchy man; his muscles were firm and hard from demanding work. He did appear older than he really was. I had no idea what he did for a living. Since this was a farming area, I imagined he worked out in the fields.

He smiled, waving his hand indicating for me to come in. "*Pase, pase.*" (Come in, come in.) Immediately, I knew this had not been a good idea. He was alone, and here I was with a man I did not know in his apartment. I wanted to turn and leave, but he went to the dining room, which was a few steps from the door, and took out a chair for me. I turned, walked to the chair, and sat down. "*Gracias.*"

With that, I began telling him why I was there and how Father Paul and I wanted to really find out the needs of our congregation. He held up his hand to his chest, excused himself for being without a shirt, he explained he had just come in from work and was resting. Withholding my apprehension and fear, I waved my hand and said it was fine.

"My name is Gualdemiro Martinez Martinez. I come from the north of Mexico; a place called Chihuahua." I took out my notebook and asked him if it was ok for me to write down his story, and he smiled as it was no problem.

"*¿Desde cuándo está usted aquí?*" (How long have you been here?) I asked.

"*Uyyy.*" He closed his eyes and laughed before continuing, "*Desde el tiempo de Regan.*" (Since Reagan's time.)

"You mean President Reagan?" I asked.

"*Sí, claro. Fue un buen hombre; no fue un gran hombre. Por él pudimos obtener nuestros papeles.*" (He was a good man. No, he was a great man. Because of him, many others and I were able to get our papers.)

"*¿Qué quiere decir «obtuvieron sus papeles»?*" (What do you mean, got your papers?)

He looked at me, quizzically. Then he scratched his head. "*¿Usted no sabe lo que es eso?*" (You do not know what that is?)

I was ignorant, "No," I replied.

"*Pues donde ha estado, Señora?*" (Where have you been, lady?) His eyes shone with mirth as he looked puzzled and surprised. How could I not know what he meant?

I recognized I had been away for many years and was not abreast of all that was going on in the country. I blushed and felt foolish. Here I was, a former professional consultant, used to dealing with government officials of other countries, and I felt incompetent and ignorant before this fellow immigrant.

"*Bueno, Señora, es una larga historia. Muchos de nosotros entramos a este país sin papeles. Sin visa, legalmente. El presidente Reagan nos ofreció legalizar y pudimos obtener permiso de estar aquí legalmente.*" (Well, Mrs., it is a long story. But many of us came to this country without papers, meaning without a visa, and entered illegally. President Reagan felt that all of us needed our legality, so he made it possible for us to obtain permission to be here.)

This was all news to me, and I needed to talk to Father Paul about this. I had no idea of the implications of what Gualdemiro had told me or its importance. They were here, as I had seen them at church, and we wanted to serve their needs. It was not supposed to be difficult. I knew nothing about the legalities of any kind. After my chat with Gualdemiro, which took longer than an hour, I decided to return to the office and ask the priest about the political ramifications that most of the church members were living in fear of every day, including Dora.

Father Paul looked at me, puzzled "I thought you knew, since you just finished working with the government."

"Father, my job was in countries answering their needs and fulfilling agreements that our government had made with their governments. I simply ran the programs. I knew something about their politics, but nothing about why people decided to move, or whether or not they were indeed moving to the United States."

"Sure." Father Paul grinned, "You were in El Salvador during the war, and many people were fleeing out of the country to seek refuge here."

"Well, yes." I acknowledged knowing that. "But why were there specifically people from Mexico? They were not running away from a war?"

"True," Father replied. "But they are fleeing hunger and a miserable existence. I have been in other countries and have seen the poverty. Some of the places' conditions are unlivable."

As I absorbed everything, I began to realize that, despite my firsthand knowledge of the countries where I worked, my focus had been on executing programs sanctioned by both our government and theirs. I hadn't spent time discussing local politics or grasping the sheer number of people desperate to leave their homeland for the United States. In the field, I witnessed the deprivation, the crushing poverty, and the injustices that shaped their lives. I believed that was why we were there—to help them push past the barriers holding them back, to give them a chance, a playing field to move forward in. And we were making a difference. Yet, it had never occurred to me that our efforts would not answer the widespread problems.

Father Paul was still talking when my thoughts went back to another program and another time. When I was in El Salvador, I remember one of our programs was with mayors of their country, and we had trained them in Florida, where they had come to learn all about being held accountable to their communities and participatory democracy. I once followed a group to San Salvador, and the President of the Supreme Court had invited me to his office. They called him "Chachi," and rumor had it that he was next in line to the presidency after President Cristiani, so I was very honored to have been invited. When I walked into his office, he steered me to another room, and there, in front of me, was a large map of El Salvador.

He waved his hand, motioning to the entire country, and said, "Diana, we have begun the reform of the Salvadoran Justice. Thanks to USAID and your efforts, we are making our mayors aware of democracy and their accountability. After living through a horrible civil war, which is huge."

And he smiled and hugged me. I was touched and felt a certain weight of responsibility I had not felt before. People like him were depending on our training to bring about the change that their country needed: to reform and better the lives of their people. There were many more programs like that, but it never seemed to be enough.

As I reflected on that moment, Father Paul's voice pulled me back to the present. "What do you think?"

I looked at him and replied, "I remember a woman, Juana, whom I had hired for domestic help, and how one day, she had told me, matter-of-factly, that her sister had left to come to the U.S. But it never registered. I never asked, how did she end up there or why? During the entire time, I had worked and lived in Latin America from 1986 to 2000, no one mentioned they wanted to come to the United States to work."

Father Paul smiled gently, "Well, Diana, you need to go home and find out what has happened all that time since you were gone. A great deal has happened, and we are now dealing with all those people who escaped the war and have come here or are from countries hungry for a decent existence."

I acknowledged he was right. He turned and left my office. "Bye now, go home and get some rest." I grinned. He was right, time to go home and rest.

When I got home that night, I took out my computer and began writing in my diary:

Like a student all these years on assignment, I decided to leave my ignorance behind and find out what had happened. I learned about the Bracero Program[1] which had started as a series of laws and agreements initiated in 1942 that lasted into 1964. The Mexican Farm Labor Agreement had been signed with the intention of supplying labor shortages caused by the war (World War II). The Mexican workers felt this benefited them since they had an insufficient harvest, and unemployment was rampant. Suzie the riveter came to the factories and made

---

1 https://guides.loc.gov/latinx-civil-rights/bracero-program

bombs, ships, and ammunition. It was the men of Mexico who came across, invited by our government, to help them work the fields. And so, we whetted their appetite for more money and an unusual way of life: Men came and went, coming during the planting season, returning to harvest, and going back home. It was a good deal for everyone. The Bracero Program was born.

It was believed to be a win-win situation. The U.S. government had men working the fields, and the Mexican government looked forward to the good wages brought back by the braceros, which would stimulate the Mexican economy. For a while, it worked well until U.S. farmers saw a way of obtaining cheap labor. Things started to get nasty when the American farmers' wages were reduced. The employers wanted to hire Mexicans because they were cheap labor, and the discrimination became worse. In theory, the Bracero Program had safeguards to protect both the Mexican and domestic farmers, but they were ignored by the greedy employers who wanted plentiful, cheap labor. According to several studies, farm wages dropped significantly between 1940 and 1950. The American farm worker decided to apply to factories and left the fields to the Mexicans. Between 1942 and 1964, 4.6 million contracts were signed, with many individuals returning several times on different contracts, making it the largest U.S. contract labor program in history.

Reading about the initial push to contract labor into the country opened my eyes to what was soon to become a mushrooming immigration problem. Here I was, in the year 2001, and we had fifty men in church celebrating mass every Sunday. Slowly, I was to learn about the Immigration Reform and Control Act of 1986 and how President Reagan tried, unsuccessfully, twice to pass this bill, but finally it was resurrected and passed on the third try. *Speaking to reporters about the bill's passage, Representative Dan Lungren (R-CA) told the media, "It's been a rocky road to get here. We thought we had a corpse. But on the way to the morgue, a toe began to twitch."* This Act alone was to be the nefarious "Amnesty Law" that so many members of the political right chant about. This law alone did enable close to three million undocumented aliens to gain status; it also enabled them to gain citizenship after five years.

Back in my office the following morning, I had my back to the door writing on the computer when I heard: "Me puede ayudar?" (Can you help me?)

Gualdemiro stood before me. He had found my office and had made his way to see me. I was pleased. He had a crisp, colored shirt, jeans, boots, and his manner was one of confidence. I assumed that if I had not visited Gualdemiro to tell him we were there to assist him and the rest of the community, he would not have come. Well, here he was.

I looked at a document he handed me, which looked like a form. "Qué son?"

He looked at me, "No sabe?" (You do not know?) He seemed surprised I did not understand him. "No," I replied, "No tengo ni idea." (I have no idea.)

"Ok," he said, "Yo le voy a ensenar." (I will teach you.) With that, he brought a chair close to my desk and put the papers in front of me. The form read: "Petition for Alien Relative."

Then, in Spanish, he said, "I want to ask for my children and my wife to come to the United States. You help me fill this out, and I can bring them. "

The form seemed easy enough to fill out. I asked the questions and wrote down the answers, and before long, we had finished filling out the form, and so filled up Gualdemiro's hope.

"Is that all you do?" I asked. He picked up the papers, thanked me, and waved with his hand, "Oh no I do other things, but sometimes I do this."

That incident was just the beginning of many, as I found myself more deeply involved with the Hispanic community. There were urgent calls to doctors for sick children, documents needing translation, and endless questions about life in our area—most of which I didn't yet have answers for. Recognizing the need for resources, I approached Father Paul about compiling a booklet with essential information. He welcomed the idea, and I eagerly took the initiative to bring it to life. As a historian, I included details about the region's past, its landmarks, and its geographic significance. My hope was to spark curiosity, to encourage people to step outside their apartments and explore. Still, I knew better than to expect much enthusiasm—people usually did not engage in activities that lacked real purpose.

The last time I saw Gualdemiro was not truly the last. Months had passed, yet he always reappeared—each time, with papers in hand, documents needing to be read and answered. I'd smile and ask, "So what do you have this time?" He'd flash a grin. "More immigration stuff." His eyes lit up, filled with the kind of pride that comes from knowing something important. Despite all my education, I still had so much to learn about immigration—a subject everyone in his world understood instinctively, a knowledge woven into the very fabric of their daily lives.

"You know, Gualdemiro," I may have sounded a bit annoyed. "I do not know if I can continue helping with this. I am not a lawyer, and I do not know what I am doing." He smiled broadly, then in Spanish, he said, "That's why I am here, to teach you."

I closed my eyes, "Oh my God, you are going to teach me?"

"Sure," he answered, matter-of-factly. "I help you help me, and then I bring my brother, and then you help others, and pretty soon you are an expert."

I could not help laughing, "So that's how it works, right?"

"Right," he smiled, and his grin was wide, and his eyes were bright. He was an eager man, a forceful man. He was not going to be disappointed. He knew what he wanted, and somehow, by hook or crook, we were both determined to unite him with his family.

He sat down, and I sat down, too. I knew this was going to be a relevant story; he was confiding in me, and I was going to listen.

"When I first came to this country, the Bracero Program was over, and I had to cross over without being detained by the border patrol. My father had come during the program, so he told me where to go and to look up the family that hired him."

"So, you just snuck in?" Gualdemiro looked at me, and I imagined what was going through his mind. "Of course," he answered. "There are guards at the border, and you have to cross when there is a shift change, or when it is dark, and you don't think they will see you."

"Isn't this dangerous stuff?" I suddenly remembered seeing war movies with soldiers crossing the enemy lines, waiting for the right moment. The difference was that we were not at war, and these were not enemy lines, just border patrol doing their job.

"No." He shook it off as insignificant. "But you do not want to get caught because they will take you in, fingerprint you, and take you back to the border and kick you out."

"So, what do you do, go back home?"

He clicked. "Nah!" He laughed. "I have crossed numerous times, and one time, they told me 'Better luck next time,' or they would tell me 'Our shift ends in half an hour, try again later.'"

I was dumbfounded. "Are border patrol always that nice?"

He shook his head, "Nah, but by and large, they are nice people. They know why we are crossing, and they are reasonable. But there are some police officers who are racists, and then things go badly."

I had heard some things about the border patrol, but I did not really want to waste time talking about them. I wanted to know more about *him*, how Gualdemiro made it across. I picked up a glass of water and gulped it down hard, then motioned him to continue, "So after crossing, where did you go?"

"Well, I had come with my brother, Rafael, and his oldest kids. Mine were too young still, and I did not want to expose them to the hard labor we were going to endure. So, we went from El Paso, we had crossed from Ciudad Juárez in Chihuahua, and walked to a house on the fourth bridge, where friends of my father lived. We ate, slept, and the next day, cleaned up and went to the farm where we were going to work for two years."

He looked down at the floor, and I felt his mind waver off. "And then, you came here?" My question jolted him back to reality. His eyes were a bit moist. "It wasn't so easy." Then, he lowered his voice. Somehow, I was on the edge of something, and he could not cross it. Even though I was anxious to know what happened next, I waited for him to recover before he continued his story.

"When we got to the place my father had worked before, down in Texas, he never told us what to expect." He looked straight at me and then turned his head away. "Have you ever heard of a short hoe?"

I was ignorant of the term. Being from Mexico City, having gone to a private American school, with a middle-class upbringing, I knew nothing about the work in the fields, so I shook my head. "Well, our boss had come from California, and back when The Bracero Program was at its height, when my father worked here, he picked up the habit of using a short hoe to get rid of weeds and for thinning crops."

"So, how did you use it?" I asked.

He got off the chair and stooped halfway, and the pain appeared so sharp he quickly straightened out. "Well, I cannot really show you, but we would stoop all the way over, bending our backs for hours. By the time you tried to straighten out, it was very painful."

I was shocked. "Oh my God, why did they make you do that?"

"I do not know, "he answered, shaking his head. "It was a way of controlling us. The short-handled hoe had an 18-inch-long handle, and you had to bend over and remain like that, really close to the ground. After two years of doing that, I almost broke my back, and I had to get out and find someone who could help me. I had lots of chiropractors try to help me, but I will never get well. I am 40 years old, and I am getting older, so as I age, and with harsh weather, I will no longer be able to work."

The moment made me cringe—such blatant control. A wave of anger and sorrow washed over me upon hearing about the injustice inflicted upon people who have experienced similar journeys as Gualdemiro had. I acknowledged his story, and in that exchange, a quiet bond formed between us. He had come to my office seeking help with something entirely different, yet he remained, sharing his past without expecting anything in return. That, more than anything, earned my respect.

I sensed that he didn't want to share anymore; the memories had long since settled into his mind like scars—etched deep with pain, too raw to relive aloud.

Glancing at my watch, I stood. "Sorry, Gualdemiro, we need to talk more, but right now, I have to speak with

Father Paul about something we're working on. Please come again—I want to keep learning about how you made your way to Indiana."

I reached out, and he timidly shook my hand, his grip light, uncertain. Then he offered a small smile. "*Bueno, hasta la próxima.*" (see you later.)

I watched him go, concern settling in my chest. His steps were slow, deliberate, his body slightly hunched, one hand pressed to his hip as if steadying himself against the weight of something unseen.

I still had a few minutes before my meeting with Father Paul, so I returned to my computer and looked up Short Hoe during The Bracero Program.

Quickly, I read an article that discussed the use of the short hoe during the 1880s, brought to California by the Chinese or Japanese agricultural workers. The tool was used as a form of oppression to keep men in check. It became a tradition that the owners of row crops, like lettuce, sugar beets, and celery, demand that their workers use these tools to be closer to the plant and more accurate in their cutting. Fortunately, the practice was not widespread. California was the leading state that used the method the most, followed by a little bit in Arizona and even less in Texas. It was a method used only in areas where plants had to be cultivated for sugar beets and other row crops.

Reading this gave me a clearer picture of where these men had been and the hardships they endured in the United States. I learned that cotton farming didn't rely on this particular harvesting method—the hoe was used for cultivating soil and removing weeds, not for pruning fruit trees or picking citrus. Other tools, like machetes, were employed for harvesting broccoli, while short knives were used to cut grapes in vineyards, where the fruit was cultivated for winemaking.

Hundreds of thousands of braceros labored tirelessly in row crops across Salinas and the San Joaquin Valley, their tool of choice—the short-handled hoe—symbolizing both their work and their suffering. As I read, I found myself shaking my head, troubled by the thought of how many men like Gualdemiro were still here, burdened with lifelong back pain, their bodies bearing the weight of years spent bent over in relentless labor.

I was deep in thought when my phone rang. It was Father Paul. "Are you coming?"

"Yes, right away," I answered, quickly closing the computer and walking over to Father Paul's office. He was writing something on his computer when I slightly knocked on the door. He looked up and grinned, "Hi, come in. Sit down."

I sat alongside his desk. "What's up?" I asked.

"I just wanted to let you know that Chief Pelter called me and informed me that Dora's husband is in jail and the prosecutor will ask for a sentence of 30 years. He has a long history of drug trafficking and other things."

I drew my breath in almost a gasp. "Wow, I did not see that coming! What will happen to Dora now?"

"I don't know," replied Father Paul. "I don't know much about immigration law, but perhaps, there will be a benefit for her, and hopefully, the ladies at the shelter will get her the lawyer she needs."

"That would be great!" I vocalized with emphasis.

Father Paul then pointed to his computer, "I am writing a grant. It is time we hire more people." I nodded, yes, we needed more hands-on board, and I would have loved a secretary. But Father Paul had other ideas, "It is time we hire someone to teach Catechism. Or could you do that?" I almost laughed and shook my head, "Oh no, father, that is not my expertise. I think it is a good idea. Do you have someone in mind?"

He smiled, "Matter of fact, I do." He leaned forward, "I met a young woman in a play I was involved in, and she speaks Spanish, actually, she was born in Mexico, but comes from American parents, came to the States to study, and is now a nurse."

"You were acting in a play?" It never ceased to amaze me how diverse Father Paul's life experiences had been.

"Oh yeah, a few years ago, I was in the charismatic movement of the church, and we did plays." He pushed it aside as not consequential and continued, "Yes, I am going to call her and see if she is interested. But I want you to meet her."

"Sure, I would love to."

"We are having a gathering with the parishioners next weekend, so maybe you can come and meet her then, sort of socially."

"I would like that. What time?"

"Oh, I guess around 6 pm."

"Ok Father, I will be there," I got up, started walking out of his office, and turned. "Could we also have someone who could assist me with the paperwork?"

"Oh, I am sure Mercy could find time to help you as well."

"No, Father, I mean, like a secretary?

He laughed. "Oh heavens, no. We are well sufficient. The three of us will be enough."

I started to feel a little irritation, but I bit my tongue. "Ok, Father, see you later." With that, I turned around and walked out of his office, feeling myself fuming. We were growing without a doubt. We had moved from our "closet" office into a building that had once been a convent, home to the religious sisters who were part of the diocese.

When we transitioned into the space, Father Paul enlisted several parishioners—men skilled in construction—to renovate it. They tore down walls, transforming the small living quarters into spacious rooms that could accommodate classes, reunions, and meetings. We even had a kitchen downstairs on the first floor. However, that level remained off-limits, as the American parishioners used it for their own activities.

Chapter 4

AND THEN THERE WERE THREE

My work at the Ministry had begun in the summer, but now, the cold was setting in. The thought of snow-covered roads and ice did not appeal to me. When I first saw snow, I was captivated—like many who come from the South—by its beauty. Freshly fallen, it was pristine, blanketing the landscape in white majesty. Back in New Orleans, snowfall was rare, almost nonexistent, so driving in it was never something I learned. Indiana, however, was a different story, and I discovered that the hard way. One particularly treacherous day, I narrowly avoided hitting a car and came dangerously close to knocking over a woman stepping out of her vehicle as I skidded to a stop. That moment left me with a lingering fear of snowy roads and icy conditions.

It was with that apprehension that I drove to the church cafeteria to meet the young woman Father Paul had spoken about. Snowflakes drifted down gently as I whispered a prayer, crossing myself, calling upon the saints and the good Lord to keep me safe. Finally, after braving the slippery roads, I pulled into the parking lot of the cafeteria, relieved to have arrived in one piece.

Throughout my life, I've encountered rare moments of instant connection with people, and meeting Mercy Campbell was one of them. She was striking—tall and slender, with auburn hair that caught the light and warm brown eyes that held an inviting depth. Her outfit, a flowing skirt paired with a well-fitted blouse and a cozy sweater, reflected both elegance and ease. But it was her radiant smile and firm handshake that sealed the feeling—I knew right away that she was someone special.

What made our connection even more remarkable was the uncanny resemblance in our backgrounds, despite the 18-year gap between us. Both of us had been born in Mexico—she, the daughter of an executive at a major American corporation, and I, the child of a top-ranking Mexican executive within an American company in Mexico City. We had both walked the halls of the American School there, pursued our higher education in the United States, then built our lives, careers, and families in this country. It was a parallel existence neither of us had expected to find.

Despite our age difference, our shared history felt deeply familiar. She had chosen nursing, dedicating herself to healing, while I had followed the path of education, guiding and shaping minds—both callings rooted in service. That we had ended up in Indiana was yet another twist of fate. We didn't know many of the same people from Mexico, but that didn't matter. What mattered was the unspoken understanding we shared—the same foundation, the same outlook on life, and a mutual desire to help others. I felt it instantly, and I cherished it.

After our initial meeting, Father Paul shared the exciting news that he had decided to hire Mercy. I was genuinely thrilled. When she arrived the following Monday, I welcomed her and led her to her new office, conveniently located right next to mine. I took some time to walk her through the space we now shared, making sure she felt comfortable and at home in our work environment.

So, how do you like the idea of working at The Ministry?"

"Oh, I love it!" She replied enthusiastically.

"Well, we are growing, Mercy, we are a very small parish, and slowly more families are starting to come to live here, so it is important to offer them catechism like Father said."

"What do you do?" She asked.

"Well, right now, a lot of different things." I let out a laugh, "I finished a booklet for families. It introduces the area they live in and what is available to them. I am also studying immigration and mostly answering their needs."

"You know, Diana, I really want to be with the Hispanic community. I missed being with Hispanics. I want to help and now feel that I can, and at the same time, continue my religious vocation.

I looked at her, quizzically, "Your religious vocation?"

She laughed. "Oh, I cannot be a nun. I am divorced and have kids. But I want to continue studying our faith and become/be more involved with the church."

"Believe me, you will see the members, and when they know you can help them with something, they will seek you out more and more."

Mercy often found herself entwined in the lives of those in need, much like Gualdemiro, who had a habit of appearing unannounced whenever he sought help. Over time, she became an indispensable support system for Maura, the mother of an autistic child named Gabriel. At first, Maura was polite and self-sufficient, but as the years passed, her dependence on Mercy deepened. Determined to help, Mercy took it upon herself to find a school where Jose could receive therapy and gradually adjust to structured learning. However, his autism sometimes led to unpredictable outbursts, posing challenges for both his classmates and teachers.

When the school called Maura to address these incidents, Mercy frequently had to step in as an interpreter, urging Maura to take an active role in her son's education. Maura, overwhelmed with two other children she considered "easier," left much of the responsibility to the school and Mercy. Understanding the complexities of autism, Mercy encouraged Maura to attend meetings and workshops with the school's professionals. It was remarkable how many resources were dedicated to Gabriel—a counselor, psychologist, main teacher, teacher's aide, and language coordinator—and it was necessary as his condition remained a challenge for everyone involved.

Though Mercy was a nurse, her true calling lay in her religious vocation. Deeply rooted in the Catholic faith, she had little patience for those who spoke inaccurately about doctrine, often finding herself frustrated by misconceptions. Lacking her depth of knowledge, I chose to step aside, listening quietly and offering my support, confident that she knew exactly what she was talking about. Her humility was reflected in her unwavering love for the gospel and her heartfelt desire to serve others.

The members of the congregation grew to care for her, and she was often invited to different prayer groups with gatherings in homes. Mercy grew to know the community in a closer manner than I ever did. I had been invited to gatherings and had gone to some but made it a point to remain close but distant at the same time. We both never allowed ourselves to become involved in their infighting or personal conflicts. "I'm not trying to be stuck up or anything," I remarked one afternoon as we were seated at our office and discussing the community. "I have learned that it is best to be kind, listen intently and try to help, but not to become involved emotionally with them, take sides or such. Father Paul is great at making their squabbles fizzle out after they discuss their differences. "

"Oh God, yes, absolutely." She agreed. "I try to visit them in their homes, and be friendly, but also try to keep myself a bit apart in order that when the sticks go flying, they are not heading my way."

"Exactly."

Coordinating the ACTS Retreats was no easy task, especially as it required Mercy to work closely with people from various backgrounds. Many participants came from small towns deeply rooted in tradition and often hesitant or resistant to change. Yet, through her unwavering dedication and the support of her assistant, she successfully encouraged more individuals to engage with the church, fostering a warm and active community. Her ability to inspire even the most reluctant participants led to a thriving youth group, while men took on leadership roles in activities like the Passion Play during Holy Week—transforming the church into a dynamic center of faith and fellowship.

Several events held deep significance within the community. Holy Week, Fiesta Latina, the celebration of the Virgin of Guadalupe, and Christmas were among the most cherished. Preparations for Holy Week began weeks in advance, with men selecting a group—including young people, women, and children—to reenact the Passion of Christ on the street in front of the church.

"Señora Diana," it was Diego, the choir leader, visiting my office. "We need to put in the bulletin something about needing young people to get involved in Holy Week."

"Ok, what do you want me to put in the bulletin?"

"Well." He scratched his head. "How about that we will have rehearsals every Saturday and after church on Sundays. You know how everyone works, and we cannot cut into that working time."

"Oh yes, I know well." I laughed. I knew it was difficult to make the members of the community participate if you were talking about weekday hours day or night. And Saturdays were possible, mostly in the afternoon.

The church bulletin had sparked interest, and soon, a participant was chosen to portray Jesus. They carefully rehearsed his lashing, ensuring it was carried out with restraint in front of the gathered crowd. As the procession moved forward in solemn prayer, their chants echoed through the church and spilled onto the streets, deepening the atmosphere of devotion and reflection.

Later, I called Mercy into my office. After our greeting, she settled into her chair, and I brought up an important matter—she would need to coordinate with the city to secure a permit for closing certain streets. As always, the city was accommodating, understanding the significance of the event.

"Is that hard to do?" She asked.

"No, just ask to speak to Duffy at the maintenance department. He will be nice and tell you what to do. Do not forget to ask them to place the street barriers so that people can walk about and get ready for the procession."

"Ok, sounds good. I will let you know if I have any trouble." She got up and walked out.

"You won't," I called after her.

The first year, the crowd was sparse—only a handful of curious onlookers lingered along the street, watching quietly. But by the second year, interest surged, and by the third, a swelling procession filled the streets from wall to wall, voices rising in chants and songs while silent prayers were whispered by those on the sidelines. What had begun as a modest gathering soon became an annual tradition, embraced by both Latino immigrants and Anglo townspeople alike.

Each year, the young Hispanics carried out the most striking moment of the reenactment—tying Jesus to a towering cross before lifting him high above the crowd. A reverent hush would fall over the spectators as they watched with solemn devotion. Some women wept, children whimpered, and all eyes remained locked on the sacred drama unfolding before them, reliving the ancient story in real time.

After a lingering silence, the crowd would gradually disperse. Soon, Jesus would be lowered, and the cross left, leaning against a large tree, draped in a flowing white scarf—a symbol of faith and reflection throughout Holy Week. It was a time of solemnity, unity, and shared worship, bringing the community together in an unspoken bond of reverence.

Time passed, and soon, preparations for Fiesta Latina began. It was late August, and Fiesta was always on September 15. I approached Mercy's desk to discuss the steps we needed to take to ensure everything was in place.

"Mercy, Fiesta Latina is coming up, and we must get ready. Father Paul always looked at it as a celebration of culture."

"Oh, do we say anything about any country. Like if it is in September that is Mexico's Independence Day, or Salvador's, and then, there's Argentina's…"

"No, no," I brushed it aside, "It was not meant to celebrate anyone's independence, but merely a time to gather and eat well, hear music, have a few dances, and chat with friends.

Since the celebration took place in September, Father Paul would step onto the balcony overlooking the street after mass and call out, "*Viva Latin America!*" His proclamation echoed through the crowd, stirring excitement. Then, everyone would make their way to the parking lot, where the air was filled with the enticing aromas of food and the vibrant sounds of music.

"Ok, so after putting the information in the bulletin, do you want me to write something about any family wanting to participate in selling food, or crafts, or stuff, need to call and purchase the space?"

"Yeah, that sounds good. How about if we charge $50 per table?"

"Hmm, yes, it sounds reasonable."

After weeks of planning—and numerous trips to the Tyson Plant to collect the chicken the women would prepare—an incident unfolded in the church's kitchen. Tensions flared as the cooks argued over what to make and who was responsible for each task. While Father Paul had encouraged them to form their own committees to promote leadership among the women, moments like this proved that fostering independence sometimes came with challenges.

Mercy handled the situation with diplomacy, and we knew better than to get too involved—otherwise, we might have found ourselves caught in the crossfire. I was reminded of something I had once heard while working in Latin America: "Everyone wants to be chief." So, we let them resolve it on their own, even when some of the tension made its way to Father Paul. Fortunately, he never gave it much weight, and, as expected, things eventually settled down.

The grand day had arrived. Father Paul and a group of men had made a trip to the monastery, where they "borrowed" countless tables and chairs for the event. Once they returned to the church, they worked together to transform the parking lot into a sprawling gathering space—tables arranged for communal dining and a large stage set for the evening's program, carefully planned by Diego and his team.

At last, 5 p.m. arrived, and everyone entered the church for mass. By 6 pm, after Father Paul's rousing call for "Vivas" in honor of every country represented, the celebration began. People wandered among the food vendors, eagerly selecting plates filled with rich, flavorful dishes before settling at the tables to eat and chat. I often took the opportunity to stroll through the crowd, visiting with families and soaking in the energy of the evening.

As night fell, the show commenced around 8 p.m.—folk dancers twirled in vivid costumes, comedians kept the crowd laughing, and Diego, ever the charismatic host, infused the event with lively entertainment.

By midnight, the festivities drew to a close. We gathered to clean up, fold tables, and ensure the parking lot was spotless for the cars that would arrive the next morning for Sunday Mass. Yet, beyond the logistics, the night stood as another shining example of the church's commitment to fostering unity—bringing together both Anglo and Latino communities in faith, fellowship, and celebration.

Another of my favorite events was the celebration of the Virgin of Guadalupe's apparition to Juan Diego in the hills of Mexico. According to legend, the Virgin appeared to Juan Diego multiple times as he tended his sheep, urging him to request that the Viceroy—the governor of Mexico—

build a church in her name. Summoning his courage, Juan Diego eventually approached the Viceroy, but his story was met with skepticism. Just as the governor was about to dismiss him, Juan Diego unfurled the mantle he always wore, revealing an astonishing sight—roses cascading to the ground and the Virgin's miraculous imprint upon the fabric. Recognizing this divine revelation, the governor's men fulfilled her request, constructing the now-famous Basilica of the Virgin of Guadalupe in Mexico City.

Each year, the celebration in Mexico City begins with a massive procession of devoted pilgrims who journey from the outskirts of the city—some on foot, others on their knees—making their way toward the Basilica. Upon arrival, they offer flowers and dances in honor of the Virgin, continuing a tradition steeped in faith and reverence.

At our church in Indiana, the celebration took place on December 12, beginning the night before at 9 p.m. The event opened with a reenactment of Juan Diego's encounter with the Virgin in the middle aisle of the church, bringing the legend to life in a solemn and moving performance. As the final scene concluded, mariachis filled the space with music, their vibrant melodies weaving through the congregation. Shortly afterward, a mass was held, uniting the community in faith and reflection.

Following the service, everyone gathered in the school cafeteria to share hot chocolate and tamales, embracing the warmth of tradition and fellowship. Events like these were more than just celebrations—they were the very fabric that held the community together, strengthening bonds through shared heritage, faith, and joy.

Once Mercy and her assistant launched the ACTS Retreats, the community's involvement in church events flourished, drawing in new faces eager to carry forward cherished traditions. Together, Father Paul and Mercy cultivated a growing parish, where participation became not only more frequent but also filled with enthusiasm and purpose. This was no longer just a place of worship—it had become home. It was their church, their priest, their sanctuary, where they felt safe and welcomed.

Regardless of what transpired beyond the church walls, inside, there was a shared sense of security and belonging. As more families arrived in the city, our office saw a steady increase in processes to assist their transition, and soon, the church began to overflow with women and children. Amid it all, I could feel Jesus' presence surrounding us, His joy unmistakable as the three of us worked to fulfill His will.

Chapter 5

SANTOS

As the three of us settled into our roles, we gradually adjusted to the increasing activity at the office. At first, the townspeople had little understanding of scheduling appointments—they simply showed up whenever they had free time, when it rained, or whenever the thought crossed their minds. Initially, this wasn't a problem. But as the community grew, the lack of structure became more challenging.

One particularly frigid winter night, I had stayed late at the office. The air was biting, and the streets were quiet when I suddenly heard a desperate knock at the downstairs door. Without hesitation, I sprang from my desk and rushed to open it. Standing there was a man, shivering violently, his clothes soaked through with snow. I quickly ushered him inside, helping him brush off the snow clinging to his jacket. Then, gently, I asked him to follow me upstairs.

He was typically short, with mahogany brown eyes, but very lean and thin. Not a lot of hair on his head, and he seemed about in his late thirties.

"Sit down, please, *siéntese*," I smiled and shook his hand. "What can I do for you?"

He handed me some papers. "A friend told me that the church lady could help me."

"*¿Oh, eso es lo que me llaman?* (Is that what they call me?) I had to laugh.

He also laughed, "*Si. ¿Es usted la Señora. de la Iglesia?* (Are you the Church Lady?)

"Yep, that is me." I took the papers and read. They were a Jury Questionnaire for the local court. I looked at him and mused. "*¿Habla usted Ingles?*" (Do you speak English?)

"*Nah, para nada.*" (No, not at all.)

"*¿Cuánto tiempo lleva usted aquí?*" (How long have you been here?) I meant how long had he been living in the United States.

Just like Gualdemiro, this man's eyes widened, "*Uyyy, muchos años, desde los 90.*" (Oh, many years. Since 1990).

"So, are you a legal permanent resident?" Then quickly, I added in Spanish, "You do not have to tell me that, but you see, in order for you to be a juror, you have to be a U.S. citizen, and I gather that you are not."

He laughed, "*Nah, para nada.*" (No, not at all.)

Again, I answered in Spanish: "Ok, what I will do is answer this questionnaire, and simply say you are not a citizen, and do not understand, speak, or read English. Sounds alright?"

"*Oh, claro que si.*" He laughed again, obviously pleased with how this was going. He looked at me intently as I began answering the questionnaire.

"Can I ask you something?" He asked cautiously.

"Sure, what?"

"Well, you see, I had an accident and I have to go to court and don't know if I need a lawyer or someone to help me, can you help me?"

I looked away from the papers and looked at the computer where my agenda was posted.

"When is it? If I'm available, I'll go with you. You don't need a lawyer for the first court hearing."

After four years in the Ministry, I had developed a solid grasp of local legal procedures. The initial hearing was straightforward—the judge would inform the defendant of their rights, explain the potential consequences of the charges, and set a future court date, at which point, they would need to appear with legal representation. I always advised defendants against hiring a lawyer for this first hearing; it was unnecessary and would save them money. When he shared his court date with me, I made a note of it in my agenda.

"Ok, I have it written down. Now, since you had an accident and you do not have a license, I would say we will meet here and then go to court." I saw he was not smiling and was anxious.

"What is the matter?"

"I do not have a car. My car was totaled."

I was puzzled, "How did you get here tonight? It is snowing!"

He put his head down, "I walked."

"You what?" I almost jumped from my chair. "Santos!" I had gathered his name from the questionnaire, "It is harsh outside. I will take you home tonight and will pick you up for your court date. I will not charge you tonight, but for your court date, I will charge you for picking you up and interpreting at court. Is that ok?"

It was as if he had been told he won the lottery. He beamed, "Oh great, *fantastico. Gracias, gracias.*"

I really wanted to know more about him, but it was late, dark outside, cold, and it was time to go home. I shut down the computer, asked Santos to sign the questionnaire, put it in its self-addressed envelope, put a stamp on it, and placed it in his hand. "Here, take this to the mailbox right outside our door. They will get it, and your obligation with the court will end."

Santos was overwhelmed with gratitude. I told him it was fine, grabbed my coat and purse, shut off the lights, and walked downstairs to the door, following him outside. On the drive to his home, I learned that he had entered the United States in 1998 and had spent years working in a restaurant. Despite his efforts to secure legal residency—the coveted "papers"—he had missed the initial cutoff date. When the deadline was later extended to April 2001, he still couldn't qualify, as he had never worked on a farm and was unable to provide the required proof. So, once again, the opportunity slipped away.

Now, in 2005, he still had no clear path to legal status. His wife and children remained in Mexico, though his eldest son had come to work alongside him. However, their relationship had soured. Manuel had grown resentful toward his father, offering little support. Santos, battling diabetes, had been hospitalized multiple times, teetering on the edge of death, yet his son had barely visited or helped. In the end, he had no one to rely on.

He looked at me and said, "Now I have you."

I was startled. "What do you mean?"

He laughed. "Yes, you will help me."

I kept my eyes on the road, "So I will," I muttered.

Those words proved to be prophetic—Santos Cruz would step into my life and never leave it again. He became a frequent visitor to the office, always arriving with a new reason to seek assistance. But at that moment, his most pressing concern was his court date.

On the court-appointed day, he met me at the office, and we drove to the courthouse together. After parking, we made our way up to the second floor, where I began my search. Moving from courtroom to courtroom, I scanned the lists posted outside each door, hoping to find his name. Finally, I spotted it on the docket for Superior Court 2—the court handling traffic violations and other misdemeanors.

We were the first to arrive, settling into the gallery as we waited for the prosecutor and defense attorneys to appear. Without legal representation, I worried the proceedings would be drawn out and uncertain. Fortunately, the judge soon entered, prompting us to rise before taking our seats once more.

He conferred briefly with his clerk, scanning the stack of case files before him, deciding which to address first. He was an older man, his hair graying and thinning but not quite bald. He wore horn-rimmed glasses and spoke in a raspy but pleasant voice. Standing at six feet tall, his presence was commanding, his black robe lending him an air of authority that was both official and intimidating.

One by one, he called out cases, questioning defendants and handing down sentences. Finally, he reached Santos' file.

"Mr. Santos Cruz, please step up to the microphone."

I got up quickly, and Santos followed, and we walked up to the microphone and podium in front of the judge. He looked at me and said, "And who are you?"

I had interpreted many times for many years in much more serious and demanding situations, so this was not difficult for me. "Your Honor, my name is Diana Palafox, I am the Deputy Director of the Hispanic Ministry of the Catholic Church, and an official interpreter. I am here to interpret for Mr. Cruz."

The judge looked over to the prosecutor, "Do you have any objections, Mr. Hartman?"

The prosecutor shook his head, "No, your honor."

"Ok. Mrs. Palafox, please tell your client to raise his right hand and repeat after me."

Once Santos had sworn to tell the truth and nothing but the truth, the judge read him the charges. Asked him if he understood. Santos acknowledged he did. Then the judge relayed the possible consequences of those charges, the time in jail or a fine. At the end, he said, "Ok, Mr. Cruz. The clerk will give you your notice of your next court date. Please be here with your lawyer."

With that, we were excused, and we left the courtroom.

"Whew," he whispered, "That was easy and fast!"

I laughed. "I told you so. Now, next time, do not come with a lawyer. In this court, the prosecutor's paralegal will come out and offer you a plea agreement. You agree that you are guilty and then pay the fine, and you are finished with the whole matter."

He looked at me, not believing it. "It is that easy?"

"Well, no, not always." I knew how difficult it could be and how often we had to scramble to find a good and not too expensive lawyer. After several years in the Ministry, I had built strong relationships and collaborated with lawyers, doctors, and service providers—public relations and follow-through became essential parts of my work. My duties often took me to courtrooms, not just in our town but in surrounding areas, as our clients faced legal troubles in different jurisdictions. Occasionally, their cases extended to other states, requiring me to write letters, obtain records, and request documents to help them navigate their legal challenges.

Most of these cases stemmed from traffic violations—primarily driving without a license. Without a valid social security number or state-issued ID, they were barred from obtaining a driver's license, which could only be granted to those who were legally present in the U.S. Though Father Paul and I never directly questioned their legal status, the reality was clear: if they didn't have a license, it meant they were undocumented---- making every traffic stop a potential crisis.

Another common issue was driving under the influence. Monday mornings at the office often brought dreaded phone calls from distressed wives and mothers whose husbands or sons had been detained over the weekend for drinking and driving. I remember losing my temper with a parent over her "lovely son," telling her bluntly that he needed to understand he was no longer living on the ranch—here, in the U.S., the law applied to everyone. If he insisted on drinking recklessly, she should leave him in jail to reconsider his choices before it was too late. Truthfully, I had wanted to tell her to let him rot in jail—but I held back. Over time, I lost patience with alcoholics who refused to take responsibility for their actions.

As I drove Santos back to the office after our court experience, and he stepped out of the car, he looked back and asked, "Will you come with me then, please?" I sighed. "Of course."

That was how it was with Santos—the neediest man I had ever encountered. Initially, I believed he had no path to obtaining an immigration benefit, but as it turned out, there were "papers" to be filled out after all. His assistance came from a woman in North Carolina, whom he referred to as a *Notaria*. At the time, I wasn't familiar with the term and assumed someone else was handling his legal process, relieving me of that responsibility. I was grateful for that.

However, I soon realized that managing immigration paperwork from a distance was anything but simple. The woman and I spoke occasionally, and eventually, I asked her to send all of Santos' paperwork so I could finalize it. Unlike most *Notarios*, as I would come to understand later, she was reliable and cooperative—she sent the documents promptly and provided helpful guidance. Once again, I found myself navigating an unfamiliar process, this time through his employer rather than through family-based immigration. I had to research and study the requirements, but thankfully, she had already done most of the legwork. My final task was straightforward—have Santos sign the remaining forms and send them off.

Months passed, and then one day, Santos burst into my office—without an appointment, as usual—waving an envelope in his hand, his face stretched into a wide grin.

"I've got it, I've got it!" he shouted, his excitement contagious.

"What?" I took the envelope from his hand and took out the letter. It was a Notice of Action from the U.S. Citizenship and Immigration Services. They were welcoming Santos to the United States; his application had been approved, and he was now a Legal Permanent Resident.

"Wow! *Que Bien!*" That was great. I gave him a quick hug. "Ok then, now you need to go to the Social Security Office and obtain your legal social number, and then from there to the License Branch and obtain your driving license. Great Santos, I am happy for you."

"You will help me, yes?" My heart sank. "Santos, all you have to do is walk in and ask for your Social Security number."

"No, you come with me. They will not listen to me, and I will get the run-around and waste time. It has happened before; you know how they are."

Unfortunately, he had been right. Even after five years in the Ministry, I still found myself fighting for people to receive the services they needed. Government offices—especially places like the License Branch—often made life difficult for immigrants. Many workers lacked a basic understanding of what it meant to be a permanent resident. They assumed immigrants arrived and quickly became citizens, never considering the long, arduous journey toward legal status. Few took the time to ask why they were here, how complicated the process was, or what challenges they faced. Some found assisting them inconvenient; others were indifferent, grumpy, or even outright rude.

But not everyone was like that. Some genuinely cared and went out of their way to help. One of them was my friend Mike, whose office was tucked away in the basement of the courthouse. As an archivist, he managed records and handled Orders of Protection. Originally from California, Mike was warm, approachable, and always willing to lend a hand. He became my trusted ally, sparing me the frustration of dealing with unhelpful clerks upstairs. Instead of sending me through tedious bureaucratic hurdles, he took care of my requests himself—efficiently and without unnecessary hassle. He was one of my favorite people.

My trips to the courthouse allowed me to build a relationship with the Clerk of Court. Though her position was political, we never discussed politics directly. Still, I picked up on subtle hints that she supported immigrants and was willing to help when needed—a fortunate circumstance, as she would soon assist me in marrying people. Yes, marrying people.

Many of our clients lived together in common-law marriages with their partners. That, as far as I was concerned, was entirely their personal choice. However, when it came to legal immigration matters, only formal civil marriages were recognized—religious ceremonies alone didn't meet the legal requirements. Beth, ever gracious, went above and beyond by officiating ceremonies with warmth and meaning. She included words from 1 Corinthians 13:4: "Love is patient, love is kind..." Standing before the couple, she led the ceremony while I stood beside her, translating each word.

The ritual gave the moment a depth beyond the simple act of signing a marriage license and exchanging a hurried "I do." It transformed the legal requirement into something truly significant. As our legal office grew, Beth continued to officiate weddings, each one carrying its own quiet beauty.

As time passed, my work in immigration increased, and I became nervous about what I was doing. I finally came to Father Paul's office one morning and sat down. "What's up?" He stopped writing and looked up.

"Father, I can't keep going like this." His smile faltered. "What's wrong?"

"Look, I helped Gualdemiro with his family's immigration process, and his children are here now—that's wonderful. But he did most of the work himself. I learned a lot along the way, but it's still not enough. And now, he's sent his brother Rafael, and more people keep coming for help. Unlike Gualdemiro, they haven't even started the process, and they look to me as if I'm the expert—the one who knows everything about immigration. But I'm not."

He crossed his hands over his lap, gazing at me directly. He knew where I was going.

"I need training, I need to go somewhere and learn."

"Funny, you should mention that," he reached for some papers on his desk. "Here, take a look at this."

He handed them over to me. A religious sister in the eastern part of Indiana had sent him information on the Catholic Legal Immigration Network. It was called CLINIC and offered training on several issues in immigration.

"As it so happens, there is a training in Dallas in a month. I was going to ask you if you wanted to go?" My eyes shone with excitement.

"Oh my gosh, yes!" I could have hugged him. This was exactly what I needed. And he was going to pay for the whole thing. Well, the Ministry was going to pay for the whole thing. I was already packing my bags and ready to go.

Chapter 6

CLINIC

I was thrilled about my trip to Dallas, never realizing how much I lacked in basic immigration law and how unprepared I was compared to everyone else there. The Catholic Legal Immigration Network, the largest non-profit immigration network in the U.S., boasts over three hundred affiliates. Its mission, *"Embracing the Gospel value of welcoming the stranger, CLINIC promotes the dignity and protects the rights of immigrants in partnership with a dedicated network of Catholic and community immigration legal programs,"* was one I deeply admired.

CLINIC offers a robust array of training programs, ranging from online webinars and self-paced courses to immersive, in-person sessions spanning two days to an entire week. I enrolled in the two-day "Introduction to Family-Based Immigration," eager to finally demystify preference categories, the Visa Bulletin, the legal ramifications of border encounters, and the thorny distinctions between misdemeanors and felonies. From the outset, the content was daunting—complex, layered, and anything but introductory. As I listened to the other attendees, it became clear just how green I was. Their questions were incisive and full of nuance, revealing a depth of experience that made me hesitate to raise my hand. Most had been practicing immigration law for at least two years. As one of the few true newcomers in the room, I felt thoroughly out of my league.

I heard about Lorna Jones, the Director of Catholic Charities in Dallas, and how she ran her office. She had earned recognition for maintaining a well-structured, highly efficient case management system. They spoke about applications for case law management, intake questionnaires, and so much more.

Then came the presentation by two nuns—an experience that completely dismantled my preconceptions about what it means to cross the border. They represented an organization that patrols the borderlands to offer humanitarian aid: food, water, and medical care to those in desperate need.

Sister Emily began talking, "Many of the nuns working at the border are not young idealists or ideologues about the poor. They are nuns in their 60s, 70s, and 80s, shaped by their own experiences, having lived in South and Central American dictatorships. They stand up for the rights of migrants as they work the border, bringing laundry detergent, baby wipes, duffel bags of second-hand clothes, and lots of water."

One attendee asked, "Sister, how often do you find dead people on the border?"

Sister Emily's expression turned solemn. "Many times," she said softly. "It is always painful to find the dead—especially the children." The room fell completely silent.

Another participant raised her hand. "Sister, can we contact you if we're searching for someone?"

Sister Emily nodded. "Of course. We're an excellent resource. We traverse the border daily and often encounter people who are lost. We cover the dry, scorching plains—where many don't survive. That's why we always carry canteens and jugs of water."

"Do you leave water along the route?" someone asked.

Sister Emily shook her head. "Not anymore. We used to. But after finding our bottles shredded by bullets, we felt such sorrow that we decided to keep the water with us instead."

A quiet voice in the crowd asked, "Why would anyone do that?"

Sister Emily didn't hesitate. "There are vigilantes who go out of their way to harm migrants—or make their lives unbearable."

Another participant raised her hand, "Could you talk about the gender-based bias that women suffer in Latin America and their escape to the U.S. southern border?"

"Many of the women we assist along the way," Sister Emily acknowledged, "have faced gender-based violence in their home countries. Many migrant women are forced to remain in Mexico, Ciudad Juárez, a city known for its femicide."

"What happens to them?" Someone asked.

Sister Michelle, the second nun, stepped in." Some women get killed, but we try to reach them and shelter them and see to it that they can cross through the main gate for an interview and entry into the country, safe from predators."

My head was still reeling from all the information. The sheer volume of new information—so much to absorb, and still so much that remained just out of reach. It was at this point, after the nuns' presentation, that one truth had settled in me with striking clarity: I needed more. I was deeply grateful to have taken these first steps, and I was beginning to realize how profoundly I loved this work. Immigration law had captured my imagination in a way few things ever had, and I found myself wondering—where had this passion been all my life? Then I remembered: I'd spent much of it navigating guerrilla territories and other heart-pounding escapades across Latin America. Perhaps those chapters were always meant to lead me here.

Dinner time arrived, and I found myself sitting next to two nuns from Indiana. They were Sister Carmen and Sister Monica. They lived about two hours away from our area, a small town called Jasper, Indiana.

"I am so glad to meet you," Sister Carmen exclaimed. "I have been meaning to call your office and ask for your help."

I looked at her, surprised, "Sure, whatever we can do, we would be happy to."

She sat down with her plate of food and put her napkin on her lap. "It's a long story to tell, I hope you don't mind."

I took a bite of my food and replied, "Not at all."

Both Sister Carmen and Sister Monica looked at each other, and I felt as if one was nudging the other, and then Sister Carmen spoke.

"Well, we have a young man, a Honduran, who came to see us. He was very scared and told us he had been kidnapped in Texas, had escaped, and was still being followed after running away from his country and being here for 10 years."

I was dumbfounded, "Did you say he has been in the U.S. for ten years? What happened?

Sister Carmen continued, "Yes, his nightmare began when some men stole cattle from his uncle's farm, and he bravely filed a report with the local authorities. The authorities were not helpful and did nothing to protect him. That single act of courage sealed his fate."

I asked quietly. "So...did they hurt him?"

The nun shook her head, her face solemn. "No, they didn't lay a hand on him, but they burned his house to the ground as a warning. It was their way of saying, *You're next*

She paused, her voice softening, "Thank God, he managed to move his wife and their young son high up in the mountains, far from the gang's reach. It's the only reason they are still alive!"

I shook my head. Then what happened? How did he decide to come here?

Sister Monica jumped in...almost as if she was reading my mind.

"Since then, the gang has unleashed relentless threats—sending gruesome images of decapitated victims and murdered bodies to intimidate him and his young wife. They gave him an ultimatum: either give them the money they had asked for, or they would find him and kill him and his family."

Then she continued softly, "Saul knew he had no choice. He couldn't provide for his family while in hiding, and the gang had already given him an ultimatum. Before he moved his family to the mountains, they had demanded more money for so-called 'protection,' And they warned him—if he didn't pay, they would find him, no matter where he ran in Honduras. They said they would torture him until he came up with the money."

She paused, looked down at her hands.

"He realized then that staying meant certain death. So, he made the heartbreaking decision to leave his family behind and come to the United States, desperate to work and send money home...praying he could keep them safe from a distance.

"In desperation, he left his family and homeland behind, hoping for safety. But safety has been elusive. He has spent the last decade moving from one state to another, always looking over his shoulder, still praying for a place where he can finally breathe and work without fear. "

"How did he get here?" I asked next.

Sister Monica picked up the story, "He left and hired a group of men that had guided others to the border of the U.S. before successfully. He trusted them."

I interrupted, "Aren't those they call Coyotes?"

"Yes," she nodded, "Coyotes."

"The problem is," Sister Carmen continued, "That when he reached the U.S. border, he was handed over to another group, and that new group asked for more money."

"What?!" I asked in disbelief.

"Yes, I know, hard to believe, right?" Sister Cermen said in disgust. "But true. And when he could not pay them because he had just given $4,000 to the first group, he had no money, they kidnapped him."

"So how did he come up with the $4,000 in the first place?" I asked.

"Oh, they sell cattle and can get money like that." Sister Monica interjected matter-of-factly.

I looked intently at her, kind of knowing where this was going. "So, what happened to him next?"

Sister Carmen stated, "They kidnapped him! They locked him up in a small house and forced him to clean and cook for weeks on end as they brought in more and more immigrants."

I was upset. I knew what this was; it was trafficking and of the worst sort.

Both Sister Carmen and Sister Monica nodded in agreement. "Yes, they kidnapped him and forced him to work all the time. They even tried to abuse him sexually."

"Oh, my goodness, Sister, that is trafficking!"

"Precisely," he exclaimed. "And that's why we wanted to talk to you."

I shook my head. "But I know nothing about the T Visa. We don't do them."

"But maybe you know of a lawyer who does?" Interjected Sister Monica.

I looked towards the ceiling, trying to remember someone. "I will look when I get back, I will try my network and see who does them. But this poor man needs help. How did he escape, or what happened to him next?"

Sister Carmen sighed. "I told you it was a long story!"

I nodded with my head, but insisted, "Please continue."

"Sister," replied Sister Monica, "I will finish the story. This really upsets Sister Carmen. So, Saul was locked up, forced work as he fought off abuse and had little time to rest, but somehow, he survived. Then one day, his torturer forced him into a car and drove him to the man's home. He gave a gun to his father and told him to guard Saul while he went to the store that was nearby to buy something. After his captor left, Saul saw the chance to run away by asking his father for permission to go to the bathroom. He went inside the house, saw the bathroom, and went out the window and ran as far as he could. He ran until he came upon an auto shop. The mechanic there helped him get away."

"Sister, what you want me to do is find a lawyer so he can file for the T Visa?" I interrupted, thinking that there was no more to the story.

"Well, yes and no," responded Sister Monica. "After his escape, which was 10 years ago, he has been running away from them ever since."

"What do you mean, running away from them?" I asked.

Sister Carmen had barely touched her food. She reached out for my hand and almost whispered, "These men must be caught and put in jail. They have hounded Saul all these years. He has run from Texas to Idaho, then from Utah to Michigan, and to Indiana. They are still forcing him to pay them. It is the only way he is keeping his family safe in Honduras."

I was shocked. I had never heard of such a thing. "I would have never guessed that criminals from another country could come into ours and continue their persecution or execution here."

Bowing her head down in sadness, Sister Carmen muttered, "Yes, and there is nothing we can do. He is staying at our Convent, safe from them, but in need of a lot of help."

"I promise you, Sister." I took her hand into mine. "Upon my return to my office, I will contact people to find the right lawyer to process his case nd see that these people are hunted down and brought to justice."

After such a wrenching story, we still managed to resume eating our meals and continued sharing our life experiences with one another. Before the night was out, we exchanged business cards with promises to get in touch.

I couldn't sleep that night. I was glad to have come to this training, to have met all the nuns, the ones who worked at the border and the ones in Jasper. I felt it was all meant to be. The whole idea of going to the CLINIC training had been purposeful. CLINIC, I quickly discovered, was more than a training organization—it was a lifeline. It served as a vital support system for newcomers and seasoned professionals alike. Among its most invaluable resources was the ability to consult directly with experienced attorneys. For us, this became an anchor during turbulent moments—especially when unfamiliar, high-stakes questions arose during client intakes. Now more than ever, this service would become nothing short of indispensable in our practice.

I was eager to return home to put my knowledge into practice, but also to contact someone who could help investigate the Saul case. I knew time was of the essence.

Upon my return from the CLINIC training, I retold the experience to Father Paul. Up to that point in time, I had been working alone, with the assistance of only my office colleagues. But now more than ever, I needed to contact someone who could help me with the Saul Ramirez case. But I did not know how.

"Diana," Father Paul suggested one day. "What you need to do is make an appointment to see one of the lawyers over at Catholic Charities in Louisville."

Change was on the horizon. A pivotal relationship with a young city lawyer was about to unfold—one that would shape my journey in ways I hadn't anticipated, spanning the years I spent within the church and beyond.

Matt Hill was a Kentuckian, a young lawyer, and head of the Immigration Office at Catholic Charities. Standing five feet 10 inches tall, stocky, with short blonde hair and piercing blue eyes, he had a way of looking at you that seemed to reach into your very soul. He dressed casually, always favoring comfort over formality. There was no pretense about him—just a relentless passion for the law and an unwavering commitment to his clients.

When I went to see him, he greeted me very graciously, and I introduced myself as the Deputy Director of the

Hispanic Ministry. I explained the reason for my visit. I told him about my work in immigration and the CLINIC training I had just had. Then I went right to the subject at hand.

"I came to see you to see if you could take a case." He smiled, and I continued, "Matt, the nuns told me the story of this Honduran man who has been subject to persecution from these criminals outside Honduras and into our country. He has suffered persecution for 10 years. Something needs to be done about these people."

Matt's deep blue eyes searched my face, and he agreed, "Absolutely. But I am not the right person. I do not do T visas. You need to go see Laura Thompson; she is a good lawyer, and she is also here in Louisville. That is her specialty."

"Oh great!" I was excited.

He turned to his computer and wrote something, then looked for some information, and turned to his printer and gave me the material he had printed. There, I had Laura's phone number, address, and information about trafficking. Later, I was going to learn that Matt always taught you or gave you material to educate you about the subject in question.

After my brief and introductory meeting with Matt, I hurried back to my office and called attorney Laura Thompson. I quickly explained the situation, and she agreed to a meeting with Saul. Then I called the nuns and told them to have Saul call me so we could meet, and I could take him to see the lawyer. They were very appreciative of my effort, and in no time, I had Saul in my office.

Saul was a young man, but I was somewhat startled by his gaunt face and thin frame. He was of medium frame, with black hair and dark black eyes. He did not look well. He was nervous, wringing his hands, and his big black eyes had a look of sadness I had not seen in a man.

"I am very grateful for your help." He said meekly.

I looked straight at him, "Glad I can help. Now, Saul," I continued, "do you have any evidence of all these texts the gangs have sent you throughout the years? Or something else?" He reached down to a plastic bag he had with him. He took out a handful of papers.

"These are some of the texts I had them print."

I took them from him and let out a sigh. It would be a great deal of pages to translate. It was obvious he did not have the money to pay for this. I couldn't help but think, "another pro bono job." Damn! After reading some of the expletives and threatening messages, I returned them to him. He took them and put them inside the bag.

"Ok, I will translate them, and then I will make the appointment to go see the lawyer. I do not know what she will do, I only know that she specializes in your type of case. Whatever she does will be of great help."

He smiled and then asked sort of sheepishly, "How much will she charge?"

I shook my head, "I do not know. When I call to make the appointment, then I will find out and I will call you back and tell you, ok?"

Saul smiled, "Ok."

"Now I suggest you remain at the Convent and not leave unless necessary. You are safe there. Whatever the lawyer does, it will put these men on the run, and they will try to get even with you. But you will be protected."

"What about my family?" He was nervous.

"Well, it would not surprise me if, along with your petition, there is another for your wife and son to come here to be with you, safely as well."

His face lit up. "Oh, that would be so wonderful! I am so worried for their safety."

I stood up, walked him to the door, and opened it. His friend was waiting for him.

"Take care, Saul. I hope this nightmare is over soon."

He smiled and shook my hand, "Me too."

I returned to my desk and called the lawyer, Laura Thompson. I looked at my agenda and agreed to see her next Friday. That would give me a week to translate.

Chapter 7

SAUL

I stepped out of the elevator, and to my right, a few feet away, was a large windowpane and a window door. On the door was a large painted sign, TOMPSON LAW FIRM. I quickly walked towards it and opened the door, and there was Saul Ramirez, sitting next to another man. Saul quickly rose to his feet and came to give me a hug. I hugged him back and stepped aside to meet the gentleman with him.

"Señora Diana, this is brother Miguel."

The man stood up, and I leaned to shake his hand. "Mucho gusto."

"Glad to meet you," I replied. Then I sat next to Saul. He seemed nervous.

"Don't be nervous, Saul, this lawyer is the answer to your prayers. I am very confident she will take care of you and your situation."

No sooner had I finished speaking than the door opened to an office in the hallway, and a young blonde, with hair in a ponytail, blue eyes, and a big smile, walked out.

"Hello, Laura. I am Diana Palafox, and this is Saul Ramirez." We shook hands, and she ushered us into her office, and we sat down.

"Don't mind me," Laura said, "I am writing down Saul's name in the file." With that, she closed the computer and turned to both of us.

"So, Mr. Ramirez, may I call you Saul?" Her blue eyes looked intently into Saul's shy gaze. I interpreted, and he answered, "Sure."

Laura had piles of papers in front of her, a laptop computer, her cell phone, and a yellow notepad. She took the notepad and placed it in front of her, and with a pen turned towards us.

"Ok. I want Saul to tell me about the years of persecution he has been subjected to, possible names of people, telephone numbers, and addresses."

When I finished translating, Saul shook his head. "No, I know nothing like that. They are the ones who have called me on my different phones. I had a phone when this all started, and through that, they talked to me, threatened me, and gave me directions as to where to send the money. It was always a store, a post office, or a phone booth. Never an address. The only thing I have had has been their phone number which was registered in my phone. After I was able to send my wife and child to a mountainous area with distant relatives, my wife told me to stop talking to them, so I threw my phone away."

"How long ago was that?" The lawyer asked, writing everything down.

"That was shortly after I arrived in Texas. After I escaped from the coyotes, I fled and, of course, kept getting their calls. But after coordinating my family's new hideout, I threw the phone away."

"That was ten years ago. So how did they find you again?" Lawyers have a very direct way of speaking and looking straight at you, making the recipient of the look a bit nervous. Saul fidgeted in his chair. "I was stupid," he replied quietly, embarrassed.

"How so?" She asked again, looking straight at him.

"Well, I had not heard from my family after about a month, and I got very nervous. I bought a new phone and tried reaching my wife, but no one could tell me where she was. In desperation, I called a friend and asked him to look for them. After a couple of days, he found them and found out they were safe. I knew later that my friend was assaulted and forced to give them my new number. After following him, they had learned the new location where my family was, and they killed him."

"How did you get that information?"

Saul looked down at the table; his forlorn look said it all. "Because they called me."

"What did they say?" The lawyer asked, not missing a beat.

"They told me that they would follow my family to the ends of the earth and that if I got rid of the phone again, they would kill them outright."

Laura stopped writing, and her gaze reached out to him as if saying, "I am so sorry."

Tears welled up in Saul's face. "I can't shake them. They call every week or send me text messages and give me directions as to how much money I need to send and to where, each time it's sent to a different place."

Laura turned and looked at me with a perplexed look. "You sent them money to Honduras?"

Saul wiped his eyes. "No, the addresses were here in the United States. Usually, a post office box. Different states all the time. After I make a drop, I am allowed to call my wife. And then I talk to my son too."

Taking it all in, Laura finished writing, and I could tell she was thinking deeply. After a few minutes of silence, she looked up at Saul again.

"Ok," She turned to me and explained that this had to be turned over to the FBI. Saul would have to hand over his phone to them. They would trace the calls and eventually find out who was calling from the States. In the meantime, she would call the State Department to see if or how they could protect someone in Honduras.

After I finished translating what Laura had said, Saul got very agitated. "No, she can't, I can't, I have to keep talking to them or they will kill my family, they told me."

Once I finished explaining Saul's agitation and concern, she understood, but had another idea. "What I need right now are the numbers that come into Saul's phone aside from the ones that have text messages. And I will hand it over to the FBI." She opened her laptop and soon made a matrix. Then she asked me to ask Saul to recite all the phone numbers that were coming into his phone. Saul looked at his phone and started to call out phone numbers and some names after them. After a few minutes, we were finished.

"Laura, now that this is going to be placed in the hands of the FBI, what should Saul do?"

She shook her head, "Nothing. He is to keep living as he has at the nun's convent, going out very little and answering their calls. Nothing is to change for now. Somehow, the FBI will hook on to his phone, and they will start monitoring the calls. Until they find them. When that happens, your wife and son are to go to another family site. In the meantime, we will have another meeting and begin the paperwork for your T Visa and to get your family here."

Saul listened intently to my translation of what Laura had said, and for the first time, I saw him smile. "Si, que bueno, muy bien. Gracias. (That is good, yes, very good. Thank you.)"

Laura stood up and shook our hands. She walked us to the door, and we bid her goodbye.

Miguel and Saul walked me to my car. I hugged Saul, "Have faith, Saul, everything will be all right, maybe not tomorrow, but soon."

"Sí, Señora. Dios la Bendiga." (Yes Mrs. God Bless You.)

I got in my car and waved goodbye. I prayed that God would bless all of us and that Saul's situation would drastically improve, and he could live a normal life with his family reunited with him here in the States. I had no idea how long the process would take, but I trusted the FBI to do the impossible.

With that, I returned to my office, knowing that Saul's case was in good hands. All I knew about T Visas and U Visas was that they took at least 10 years to process, only because there were so few visas for those categories, something like 10,000 a year, compared to 220,000 for others.

A week after my visit with Saul at Laura Thompson's office, I had to go to Louisville to meet a client that I was to interpret for at Matt's office. It would give me the opportunity to thank Matt for the referral of Laura.

Matt's staff was always friendly. We usually chatted until my client arrived, and Matt could see us. Once my client arrived, we waited a minute or two, and then Matt opened his office door and invited us in.

"How did it go with Laura?" He asked, as we sat down.

"Oh, she was great!" I answered. "I am very confident she will help Saul and his family."

"Glad to hear it." He turned to my client, and I introduced them. Then, I quickly discussed the client's situation and waited for Matt to begin his consultation.

Matt was known for his long appointments, but there was a reason for that. During an intake, he meticulously uncovered everything he needed to know, ensuring his clients had sound and practical options. I admired how, by the end of each session, he would present two or three solutions, written out clearly so the client could understand their choices. His patience was a defining trait—unless he sensed deception. When a client tried to mislead him, the flush of red that crept up his face was a clear warning. In those moments, I knew trouble was brewing. Matt had no tolerance for dishonesty, and he had a way of making clients backtrack until the truth finally emerged.

Every session with him was a lesson—not just for the client, but for me. There was always something new to learn, and time spent with him never felt wasted.

That afternoon, after saying goodbye to my client, Matt turned his intense gaze on me. "Diana, you need to become an Accredited Representative," he said. "You're practically practicing immigration law illegally."

His words were direct, weighty—impossible to ignore.

I looked at him, shocked. "What does that mean?"

"Easy, get a hold of your field coordinator at CLINIC, and they will help you out. You have their website, look it up."

"Oh Matt, I don't know, I feel I need to know so much more!"

"Exactly!" he leaned across the desk and looked at me intently, "You know more than many lawyers practicing law that are not immigration lawyers. Just build on that knowledge and do it."

Matt was right. I knew it was time to move forward. By 2009, I had spent eight years immersed in immigration work, and we had seen real success. We—Mercy, Father Paul, and I. Mercy helped when she could, though her responsibilities within the church kept her busy. The First Communion classes had expanded, drawing in more volunteers to assist with catechism. She had also started a prayer group and was considering traveling to St. Louis,

Missouri, to learn how to lead an Acts retreat. It involved getting men and women into discipleship and learning how to involve others in the church.

With Mercy's support in ministry, my efforts in immigration and social services, and Father Paul's charismatic leadership, the church was flourishing. I often pushed for hiring a secretary, but Father Paul was hesitant.

I began to attend more CLINIC's seminars to become an Accredited Representative—two-day workshops, intensive week-long trainings—traveling to Kansas, Missouri, Michigan, Texas, Washington D.C., and Louisville, Kentucky. With each training, I gained more knowledge, equipping myself to better assist the immigrants who walked through our office doors.

After returning to my office from one of my training trips on Naturalization and the process to become a citizen, I had a group of five men waiting to meet me. They wanted to become citizens. Could I help them? *Oh, my goodness*, I thought to myself, "God, you are funny!" Here I was with an M.A. in Latin American Studies, and an ABD in Latin American History, one of my favorite courses had been American History, and I was becoming a buff devotee of the Founding Fathers and Constitutional Law. And I just had this one-day training on the Form N-400, all about naturalization. It would be easy to teach them and prepare them to become citizens. Silly men, of course I could help them!

I decided that the perfect time to have a captive audience was on Sundays, right after Mass. I taught in one of the largest rooms on the second floor, and when I walked in for the first time, fifteen men sat before me, smiling and eager to learn. This would be my first time teaching U.S. history in Spanish.

I knew that U.S. Citizenship and Immigration Services preferred history instruction to be in English, but if I followed that rule, I wouldn't have any students. So, I devised a way to integrate both English and history, helping them not only grasp historical concepts but also build their language skills to confidently answer questions on the application.

Before the changes in 2008, aspiring citizens had to memorize one hundred history questions and learn to write one hundred sentences in English. I structured the course as a 14-week journey through history, weaving in Mexican and Latin American narratives where they intersected with the U.S. story. To my surprise, many of my students weren't familiar with their own country's history, so every lesson sparked excitement.

The classes were highly interactive, with vibrant discussions that often stretched beyond the allotted time. After wrapping up the material and guiding our conversation for about an hour and a half, I'd glance at my students, still seated, waiting for more. I'd smile and gently remind them, "That's all for today. I'll see you next week."

By then, after long days and busy weeks, all I wanted was to get home and rest. I'd gather my materials, wave goodbye, and step out of the room, already anticipating our next session.

My students came from diverse backgrounds. Few had attended college; most had barely completed grade school, having grown up in remote villages with limited access to formal education. Yet, despite their circumstances, some possessed sharp, inquisitive minds, capable of crafting compelling arguments.

After 14 weeks of discussion and participation, many stayed on for an additional two months to refine their English-speaking and writing skills. Their thirst for knowledge was undeniable, and it was why they loved my classes—I wove their own country's history into the narrative, making every lesson personal and relevant. When we discussed democracy, we compared systems, examining the contrasts between the United States and their home countries. While no one spoke too personally, some hinted at hardship, even persecution.

I was continually inspired by their determination—their relentless drive to learn, to really overcome language barriers, to build a future despite the obstacles before them. One moment, however, stuck with me. A man approached me, hesitant, fearful. He wanted to apply for citizenship but was paralyzed by doubt—he could not read or write.

His vulnerability spoke volumes, and in that instant, I understood the profound weight of what it meant to *want* a new life but feel unworthy of it.

"*Señora*. Diana, I am not learned. I did not go to school, so I do not know how to read or write."

I looked at him straight in the eyes and said, "That is not a problem. I will teach you. All you need is to want to do is learn."

I was quite taken aback that he could not read, but I resolved to help him. He committed to coming every day, late afternoons, and for months, I taught him how to read and write in English. It was easy to teach him how to read and write in Spanish afterwards. It took us a year, but eventually he went for his interview and passed. When he came to see me, he and his wife had a basket full of tamales. I gave them both great hugs, it was the best way of thanking me. I have to say, during my time in the church, I acquired many gifts: purses, dolls, ceramics, paintings of the Virgin of Guadalupe, embroidered hankies, pillowcases, candies, and so on. It was their way of saying "Thank you."

Another very memorable event was the first citizenship ceremony I attended. It was for the first class of fifteen men. It took place in the Indiana State Capitol, on the second floor of the courthouse. As I stepped into the courtroom, I was struck by the grandeur—the soaring ceiling adorned with Italian Renaissance paintings, the marble banisters gleaming under the soft glow of overhead lights. The space exuded importance, a fitting backdrop for the momentous occasion unfolding within its walls.

My students arrived in their finest attire—with suits, crisp white shirts, neatly knotted ties. Their shoes polished; hair carefully slicked back. They all stood tall, embodying the pride and dignity that such a ceremony required. Some had brought their wives and children, who sat in the gallery, wide-eyed, taking in every detail of the ceremony. To them, this was not just a legal formality; it was a milestone, a major transformation.

I watched as men, hardened by years of struggle, broke down in tears upon receiving their certificates. Their gratitude was boundless. They embraced me tightly, their eyes shining with emotion—proof of how deeply this moment mattered.

I often found irony in the judge's words: "*Welcome to the United States, you enrich the fabric of our society.*" But at the same time, I cherished them. I was as proud of these men as they were of themselves. They had worked tirelessly for the achievement, and they knew—perhaps more than many born into citizenship—what it truly meant to *belong* to a country. They consciously had chosen to become citizens.

As I stood among them, I couldn't help but wonder: how many of our own—young and old—truly understood our nation's history as deeply as they did? How many loved this country with that same unwavering devotion?

As my classes continued, I decided to start a new session with a minimum of five students. Often, they wouldn't call ahead or schedule a meeting—they would simply show up, eager to learn.

Over the years, I shifted my classes from Sundays to Saturdays, holding them from 3 p.m. to 4 p.m. By that time of day, most people had finished work if they had Saturday shifts, making it the perfect window for studying U.S. History and Civics.

What began as classrooms, filled exclusively with men, gradually evolved in that, as time passed, more women joined, and eventually, the classes reached a balance—an equal mix of men and women, each contributing their own perspectives and experiences.

In one of my earliest sessions, a tall Mexican woman—about 5 feet 8 inches—walked into class. She wore a long skirt and a crisp white blouse, her ebony-black hair piled high in a bun atop her head. Her fair skin contrasted with her striking green eyes, which carried an expressive intensity. She had a sturdy frame—not overweight, just built with the strength of someone who had spent years tending to a family and carrying responsibilities.

Later, I learned that she came from Jalisco, one of the more diverse states in Mexico. Many of its people are green-eyed, and some even red-haired, as a result of many foreigners coming to live in that state. She had five children and had married her childhood sweetheart. From the start, she made it clear that she was coming to class *for* her husband. I didn't understand what she meant—he looked American. I assumed she was learning to please him, to support him.

But as the weeks passed, through study sessions and class discussions, I uncovered the truth. Raquel's husband was undocumented. The revelation stunned me. He looked so unmistakably Anglo—he spoke English fluently, was six feet tall, with sandy hair and deep green eyes. He sounded and looked like an American.

I was intrigued. Though I never pried, never asked personal questions, I couldn't shake the curiosity. What was his story?

"Well, it was because he came when he was a kid, then left a young man and came again. He even went to school and finished High School in Texas."

"When did you meet him?" I asked Raquel.

She laughed and answered coyly, "Oh, he was the assistant to the pastor in our church, and every time he came back, we would talk. I fell madly in love with him."

She grinned widely. "We married when I was 15!" With that, her eyes lit up.

I had to laugh. "Goodness!"

She rambled on, "I was still in school, and our parents chaperoned us, and finally, he asked me to marry him, and I could hardly wait, so I said 'yes.'"

"How did you come then to the States with your legal residence, and why doesn't he have one?"

She laughed, "Because my father applied for us, all of us, my mother and all my siblings and me. We all came in legally. After marrying him, I waited a few years and then applied for him."

"So why isn't he a resident now?" If she applied the latest at her 18th birthday, his process should have been done years ago.

"I don't know," she answered, "That's why I am going to become a U.S. citizen, bring his case to you, and hurry this up."

I was concerned she had mentioned that he had come and gone several times. That was a red flag. I would have to know later exactly when he had first come across the border, what had happened at his crossing, how old he was, among other information. She promised to call and make an appointment for my interview with him, but many years would pass before I heard from her again.

Over the years of teaching U.S. civics and history to future citizens, certain students left a lasting impression on me. Two women stood out above the rest. One of them was Maricela Gomez.

She had recently arrived from Mexico and was a legal resident. Because her husband was a U.S. citizen, she would be eligible to apply for citizenship after three years of residency. Yet, in those three years, Maricela had spent most of her time isolated, confined within the walls of her apartment—rarely meeting new people, rarely venturing out into the community.

Then, one day, something shifted. Determined, resolute, she made up her mind: she was going to learn English. She was going to pass her citizenship test.

And so, her journey truly began.

"Señora Diana, I know that with your help, I can master this."

I looked at her and, upon realizing her resolve, I smiled. "Of course, you will."

For two years, Maricela was always on time to class, and she arrived with her husband by her side. She always asked questions and had strong opinions. Her husband would just smile and sometimes pat her arm to calm her down a bit. She felt comfortable and in a safe place to speak out and say what was on her mind. I was quite taken by her common sense and intelligence. She had grown up in a small town, had never left her town other than to go into the big city, and had never left her country. And here she was, in another country, with a huge language barrier, determined to succeed. She was small, about 5 feet 1 inch, and had long black hair matching her large, doe black eyes. As time passed, Maricela became the star student and gained the respect of all her peers. I could not go to all the citizenship ceremonies, but Maricela's was one of the ones I did not miss. She was an example for many. Word got around in her own social circle that if Maricela could pass the test, any woman could too. That is when I began to see more women step up after their husbands had become citizens. What had kept them afraid was the language, but as they came, tried, and learned, they gained the confidence they needed to become citizens.

If I ever had a client tell me they could not study and pass the citizenship test due to their lack of language, I would take them to the board where I had photos of some of my students who had passed. One photo on the board was of a Muslim woman.

I pointed to her, "She is from Jordan, and spoke no English at first, and I did not speak Jordanian at all. But she wanted to learn and wanted to become a citizen so badly that she brought her husband to our one-on-one classes. He was the interpreter." My student's eyes widened.

"And, he helped her understand you?" A student asked.

"Yes, he did. And after two months, she took her citizenship test and passed it! So, you see, with effort and the desire to do it, anyone can study, learn, and pass the test."

It was a difficult argument to refute. Students continued signing up, and classes carried on. Yet, I couldn't shake my frustration that we were never able to apply for the grant offered by the Department of Homeland Security. That particular funding could have significantly eased our financial burden, but the requirement to teach and prepare one hundred students per year was simply unreasonable.

Language acquisition isn't quick or simple—it could take years, seven to ten years before someone becomes fluent. Expecting us to successfully train a hundred students annually was unrealistic, especially when many were learning English from scratch. The most students I had ever managed to teach was sixty-five in a year. The grant totaled $250,000 over two years—had we met even half the requirements, we could have secured half the funding, making our work much more sustainable. That would have allowed us to expand our services.

Running a ministry—and later, a nonprofit—meant constantly grappling with financial uncertainty. Every two weeks brought the same headache: realizing there might not be enough funds to pay the staff, who worked tirelessly filling out paperwork and accompanying clients to appointments. With Father Paul, however, the financial strain was far less severe. He had a remarkable ability to rally the community and secure the funding we needed.

I still remember the day he called me into his office, and he showed me a check he had just received. It was made out to our ministry, and the sum was $15,000.

"Wow," I said. He smiled and swiveled in his chair. "Yeah, that is a good guy. He sends me money every year. He believes in what we are doing, and it is his way of showing it.

"How many of these do you get?" I asked.

"Oh, not many, but enough to keep us going. And of course, I write grants, and that helps."

He was right, I did not feel the burden and pressure of running an office and seeing that it had all the money it needed to function. Father Paul would make it look almost easy. I was so involved with the legal side of our office that I never questioned or worried about how we would be able to continue our work. It would be years before the Ministry would close, but I took on a non-profit and found out how hard it was to keep it all afloat.

Chapter 8

GABRIELA

Becoming an Accredited Representative was a journey that required years of study and months of meticulous preparation. There was an extensive list of documentation to submit, followed by a cataloging of webinars, one-on-one training sessions, and certificates. Thanks to a generous donor, our office acquired a law library—an essential resource, as our "Agency," itself, needed accreditation. The process was tedious and painstaking, requiring every detail to be perfect—every "i" dotted, every "t" crossed, all necessary documents and letters of recommendation secured.

The happiest day came when I received the official letter in the mail: I was now a Board of Immigration Appeals Accredited Representative. With this credential, I could provide legal advice, represent clients at the immigration office, and advocate for them with ICE and other agencies—though court appearances still required an attorney. For legal representation in court, I always relied on Matt, my lawyer friend from Louisville.

By 2009, we welcomed a volunteer from the community who was eager to improve her Spanish while assisting with immigration work. Until that point, I had been working alone, struggling to keep my head above water as more and more people sought help with their paperwork. Now, I was guiding men through the process of bringing their wives and children to the U.S. via the Consular Process—a vital pathway that united families but required careful navigation.

Having a volunteer was a challenging experience, especially in the training phase, and in terms of time management. When Ann McLean expressed interest in immigration work, I was thrilled. My previous volunteer—a hopeful candidate from another parish in Louisville—had become overwhelmed by the complexity of the procedures and ultimately backed out after training, leaving me feeling as if precious time had been lost.

Ann, however, was different. She wasn't just enthusiastic—she was proactive. She dove into law books, studying them on her own, and diligently absorbed knowledge. Over time, she built a solid understanding of immigration law. My only concern was that while she mastered the legal concepts, she wasn't in the office often enough to engage with clients and learn through hands-on experience—an essential element in truly developing confidence and effectiveness. To excel in this work, you need both knowledge and practical application. One without the other isn't enough.

Ann was an immense help and a happy person to have around. Her positive attitude and belief that all would pan out really helped in the dark moments when we thought the world was closing in on our community.

Our moment of trial came when we received word from a lawyer in the AILA (American Immigration Legal Association) list-serve that it was imminent that ICE (Immigration Customs Enforcement) was going to come in full force against neighborhoods and companies searching for people to deport. We felt impotent and only found that assisting people with custodian/guardianship letters would relieve the concern of leaving children behind if deported. Immediately, I asked Ann to start calling people and making appointments to fill out affidavits designed by a collaborating lawyer that would give citizens or resident relatives the guardianship of the children if the parents were deported.

We had two other nonprofits reach out to us and ask what they could do. Well, we were not about to hide anyone, so really, there was not much to do except help families prepare in case something happened. As usual, we called for and received the professional assistance of our lawyer friends. It was amazing how the Anglo community rallied to help. Whatever was being said by politicians or the news, there might be racism and ill feeling towards immigrants, but the real people, the people we worked with and were part of our community, wanted to help and made themselves available for whatever was needed.

The warning was frightening and put us on alert, but nothing happened. We later found out that ICE had decided not to do it. But in the meantime, many in our community had come to reassure themselves that their children would be taken care of in case of a dire situation. The biggest fear parents had was to be detained and not be able to send word to their children and arrange for someone to pick them up from school and take them home. Once home, take care of them.

Some of us committed to signing guardianship letters where we committed to taking their children to Mexico, to them once they were deported. It was a tough call, but we were committed to helping our community.

Ann surprised me when she let me know that she and her husband were willing to do that for a couple of families they had gotten to know. She and her husband were generous towards members of our Latin community. Ann was an Anglo with some German blood and a good mix of Irish in her, all blonde, blue-eyed, middle-aged, small, framed lady. She and her husband who was Italian descent, were retired and did consider themselves serious "birders" (people who go out and sight birds and write down where they found them and what species they are, etc.). She gave a great deal of her time, and we were grateful.

Even Father Paul became deeply involved. He had signed guardianship papers for two families, and we spoke about it at length. Years earlier, he had taken a yearlong sabbatical, traveling throughout Latin America to visit the homes and families of the people who attended our church. The very idea that their priest—their *padrecito* (an affectionate term)—would travel to their hometowns, meet their parents, siblings, and extended family was breathtaking. It was a gesture that meant the world to them.

For Father Paul, it was an opportunity to form a deeper bond with his parishioners, to meet the loved ones they had left behind, and to witness the hardships they endured. It felt only natural for him to sign guardianship papers for families he had come to know here *and* in Mexico. The relationships he built between the members of our church and their families back home were extraordinary. He had even been invited to celebrate mass in their town churches, an honor that spoke to the trust and affection they held for him.

As a Franciscan priest, Father Paul embraced the humility that defined his order. He never sought recognition, accolades, or excessive gestures of gratitude. He carried out his work with quiet devotion and unwavering love, asking for nothing in return but faith in God and heartfelt worship.

I learned a great deal from Father Paul. If our beginning had been a little rocky, as time passed, we learned to appreciate and respect each other. Quite honestly, I loved him as my spiritual guide, the one person I could totally confide in and who could set my fears at ease. He was truly a man of God. I had often wondered why Father Paul had taken his vocation as a priest and not married. He was very handsome, had green eyes and brown, greying hair. He was very lean, tall, and had an athletic body. The best part of Father Paul was his smile. When he smiled, his eyes shone, and you knew he was pleased with whatever you had done.

The fear of imminent apprehensions and family separations gradually faded, and soon, no further mention was made of the ordeal. We felt a sense of relief knowing that a significant portion of the community had secured guardianship papers—ensuring that, in a worst-case scenario, their children would be protected. With this burden lifted, we refocused our efforts on preparing families for their upcoming interviews in Ciudad Juárez, Mexico—an essential step in their journey to legal permanent residency.

Once approved by the U.S. Consulate in Ciudad Juárez, applicants could legally re-enter the United States and reunite with their families, bringing an end to years of uncertainty. The prospect of a long-awaited legal status filled them with hope, reinforcing our commitment to guiding them through the process.

Then, Gabriela came. Gabriela Rendon had reached the end of her Consular Process. She had gotten her appointment in Ciudad Juárez to go for the interview that would either deny or give her legal residence, to return to her family. The Consular Process begins in the United States, and the petitioner is usually a spouse, parent, child, or sibling. In Gabriela's case, it was her husband, Rafael Huerta, who had petitioned for her. He was a U.S. citizen, born in El Paso, Texas, of a Mexican immigrant family. They had five children, and the smallest was 2 years old. Little Geovanni clung to his mother as we sat going over the orientation to her trip.

"So, are you taking Geovanni with you?" I asked since, as a dependent, the child was with his mother.

She lowered her eyes and smiled at her son. "No, I am leaving him here with Rafael."

"Oh my," I sighed, "Won't that be hard?"

She looked at me with sad eyes, "The whole thing is sad, Señora Diana."

"I know, but leaving little Geovanni... how will Rafael do?"

Tears ran down her cheek. "The question is, how will I do, away from all of my children, including this little one?"

She had a point, and there was not much I could say. Fortunately, the system had changed so much, thanks to the Obama Administration. Before, any person who returned to their country for the interview at the U.S. Consulate would have to wait months after the interview to see if they were given the approval to return. Some had to stay months, and one of my families had to wait three years. I can still remember the young wife with tears in her eyes, begging me to help bring her husband back. This was an area where we could not do anything; we had no control. It was up to The Consulate adjudicators to decide the fate of many of our clients. It was not always based on the law; rather, it was based on the criteria or personal decision of the adjudicator.

It was 2009 and the Obama administration would place Form I-601A for Grounds of Inadmissibility until 2013. That new procedure was going to allow people to wait and remain with their families until the waiver was approved and then travel to their home country and appear for their consulate interview. In a week to 10 days, families could be reunited. Gabriela was not going to be so lucky. She might have to wait perhaps one month, weeks or years.

Gabriela was hoping to return in two weeks at the latest and be reunited with her family to live happily ever after.

But there were no assurances, and I never gave them any guarantees. All we could do was our best.

"Well, you know Gabriela." "I looked directly at her to try to reassure her of the reason your waiver was approved. "It was because you were seeking a pardon based on the hardship Rafael would experience with his ill health, being in charge of five children and a full, fast-moving, and successful business. He was going to worry about the caretaker he would have to hire before you left, and then at work, worry, and then worry some more about where you are going. Michoacán is one of the worst and most dangerous places in Mexico right now." She wiped her eyes with a Kleenex I offered, and she moved her head with agreement. "But it is still hard," she said softly, "leaving the children and then, little Geovanni and traveling alone, not knowing what will happen. It is all very scary."

"Rafael is not going with you?"

"Oh no, he must remain and look after the kids and his business. The construction business is always busy, and there are always problems with the workers. Rafael's group is all Hispanics, and they must work with the contractor's group, and sometimes, there are problems. "

"Like what?" I asked..

"Uyyy." She sighed. "The Anglos, the whites, sometimes do not show up to work, and Rafael's men must do their work, and it gets a bit tense. Or there is discrimination in subtle ways, and that causes friction. Or sometimes, Rafael does not get paid."

"What do you mean?"

"Well, we had to hire a lawyer and go to court because this one contractor decided to pay half of the job and then said he was not happy with something and simply did not pay him, and Rafael had to pay off his men out of his own pocket. It was very trying for him."

"Did he win his case? Did the contractor pay him?" I asked.

Gabriela had gotten excited, and her eyes lit up as she said in disgust," Yes, we won, but our lawyer had to garnish the other's wages, and it was a tough fight. Sometimes, I think that having a business and doing business with whites is not good."

I was later going to learn that this sort of thing happened frequently. Being an immigrant, and specifically, a Hispanic, meant everyone thought you were illegal, and therefore, anyone could cheat you. Rafael was a citizen, but no matter what, he had to prove the worthiness of his work and fight to get paid for it. Years were going to pass when this sort of discrimination was going to be more and more common among our parishioners, and our agency was going to fight this and try to win every time. The general friendliness the Anglo community towards immigrants and Hispanics, at the time, was good and all was well, but it was not going to last.

Getting away from the conversation of how her imminent trip had revived her, I had to steer it back to the orientation at hand.

"Ok Gabriela. Here are the documents that the Clinic will ask for." I laid it all in order, with each pile of papers properly marked. This one had a Post-it that said CLINICA.

"Now, after your medical exam, where they will do X-rays of your lungs, and they will draw blood to see if you have tuberculosis. Then they will immunize you for Rubella, Measles, AIDS, and other vaccines. I cannot remember all of them."

Gabriela was very attentive. She took the documents and placed them in a folder.

"After your medical exam, Jose Luis, our agent in Juarez, will take you to the ASC (Application Support Center) where you will provide your fingerprints, photograph, and sign something. They coordinate with The Consulate, where you must go for your interview."

I reached out and placed several documents in a small pile, with a post-it ASC. "This has your appointment letter, a copy of our appointment with them, a copy of your DS-260, your biography, and a copy of your passport. They will submit all of that to The Consulate and then, after a day or two, you go to your consulate interview, and you will hand them this packet." Again, I reached for the one marked "CONSULATE." "Here is the appointment letter again, your birth certificate and those of Rafael's and your children's, as well as your original Waiver approval and, most importantly, a copy of your Affidavit of Support." Her eyes followed closely my organization of her documents.

I continued. "The Affidavit of Support is a document that explains to the government how much money Rafael makes, and it is accompanied with his birth certificate, your tax return for this year, and a letter stating he is self-employed. It tells Uncle Sam that you will not be a burden to the government. That neither you nor Rafael will ever seek financial help from the government. "

Gabriela shook her head, "Uyyy no, we would never seek help. Rafael makes good money, and I hope to start working too. We will be fine."

"Ok, Gabriela, do you have any questions or doubts?"

Once again, her eyes widened, and then she lowered her gaze, "What if I am not allowed in? What if I cannot return?"

I looked at her directly and gently said, "There is no reason you should not be allowed back in. We have done all the proper procedures, handed in all the principal documents, and you do not have a criminal background or have done anything that could keep you from coming back. Why do you feel this way?"

"It's because I have heard about other people going and not coming back at all or having to stay down there for years."

I had heard this so many times. People in the community liked to talk and always included everyone's case as their own or someone they knew. I assumed it was so that they could feel important or simply because they were totally misinformed. This usually made me frustrated. However, Gabriela needed assurances, not my frustration. I sighed deeply and explained.

"Look, Gabriela, everyone's situation is different. There are rules and laws that will keep some people from coming back because they may have done something illegal, sometimes without knowing, many years ago.

Unfortunately, what some people do many years ago will follow them regardless of how long ago it happened."

I knew this to be a fact because I had many clients who, when asked about perhaps having a previous brush with the law, would wave their hand and say, "Uyyy, that happened many years ago." There was a general belief that the passing of years would erase the legal problem. It did not. Records are kept, and when fingerprints are given, the FBI will find out.

I looked at Gabriela and saw that I had made her less worried. But there was still something in her facial expression that troubled me. "Is there anything else you want to tell me? Or any other doubt you have?"

She looked down to pick up her purse, got out of her chair, and collected the documents and the large packet I had given her. "No, that is all. Thank you so much for everything." With that, I came around and gave her a hug, looked her in the eye, and said, "Everything will be alright."

She smiled, "Si," and she left the room. I sat there, feeling uncomfortable. I could not put my finger on it, but it was a feeling I had. And not a good feeling. I shook my head, *It's nothing*, I thought to myself. *She will be fine.*

The events I read about the night before weighed heavily on my mind—an article detailing a brutal killing in Ciudad Juarez during the September 16th Independence Day celebrations. Drug cartels waged violent battles, showing no regard for bystanders caught in the crossfire.

The article described a massacre at a drug rehabilitation center, occurring just as President Felipe Calderón rang the bells of freedom, marking the 199th anniversary of Mexico's independence from Spain. The chilling account painted a gruesome picture—walls riddled with bullets, pools of blood, bodies everywhere. Between ten and thirteen lives were lost in that single attack, pushing the month's death toll to three hundred, solidifying Ciudad Juárez's grim reputation as one of the bloodiest cities in the world. With each passing month, the tally rose, driven by relentless gang executions.

Despite the army's presence and Calderón's bold declarations that Ciudad Juárez would serve as a "national model" for combating drug violence, the carnage showed no signs of slowing down. I worried deeply for the families forced to risk their lives in order to complete the Consular Process, the only path allowing them to legally return to the U.S. and reunite with their loved ones.

I hoped and prayed that Gabriela would remain safe. We were fortunate to have Jose Luis—an exceptional agent—who, alongside his wife, looked after our clients, ensuring their well-being. I thanked God for placing him in our path, for making it possible to provide security and guidance in a situation fraught with danger. So far, we had been lucky. No one had been harmed.

Then we got the call from Rafael. Days had passed, and we were expecting to hear from Rafael that Gabriela had gone through the process without any problems and was on her way back. He informed us that they had not allowed her to return because they doubted his citizenship.

"What?" I was aghast. "You were born in El Paso, you have a certificate, what was the problem?"

Rafael's gaze met mine, and he was angry, his black eyes darkened, and he furrowed his brow. "It is because my birth certificate is from El Paso that they do not believe it."

"What do you mean?"

"Well, evidently, there have been some women who gave birth to children and then crossed over to the U.S. and had midwives certify that the child was born in the United States."

"What is it that they want you to do?"

"To prove that I was born here."

I was amazed. I was amazed not that immigration would question his nationality, but that there had been women who had done such a thing just to have a child born in the U.S. I really did not believe it. Worse still, we had to help Rafael prove it, prove his citizenship, and help Gabriela return. All I could think of was two-year-old Geovanni crying in her arms. Immediately, I tried to put Rafael at ease and told him we would find out how to prove his case with authentic documents that would give him credence.

After he left, I called Ann into my office and explained the problem.

"Oh no, Gabriela and her little one, they were so sweet." Ann cried out. "What can we do?"

I had the file in front of me. I started to sift through the papers and thought that what we needed was the hospital certificate. Usually, when a baby is born in the States, the hospital offers a certificate with the baby's name, the name of the parents, and the baby's foot imprint. That would be perfect.

"Ann, call Rafael's family; he has a brother in town, and find out if he knows which hospital his brother was born in. Try to talk to other members of Rafael's family and try to find out everything about his mother and his birth. And we need to act fast. Gabriela will not be allowed back until this is settled."

I returned to my computer, determined to find more information about whether the practice existed babies born across the border and later, brought into the U.S. to seek citizenship. The idea seemed almost fantastic, even far-fetched.

Then, I stumbled upon a Washington Post article from September 2009. According to the piece, a State Department official had stated that there had been no change in policy or practice regarding the adjudication of passport applications. However, they acknowledged that the U.S.-Mexico border region had seen a significant incidence of citizenship fraud. The burden of proof seemed to fall on individuals born between the 1950s and the 1990s.

I turned my attention to Rafael's birth certificate. Born in 1983, he was now 35 years old. As I examined the document, searching for anything that might provide clarity, the phone rang. It was Roberto—Rafael's brother.

"Hola Roberto." I greeted him, "How are you?"

"I am good, *Señora* Diana, you called about my brother Rafael?"

"Yes, Roberto, do you know what the name is or where the hospital your brother was born in is?"

"Oh, he was born in a hospital, but the hospital burned down years after my mother had given birth to my brother."

"How? When?" I was grappling with the news and trying to find a way to help.

"I really don't know. After my mother gave birth to my brother, she stayed with her sister, my aunt, who was her only recourse. She had crossed months earlier and had to seek her help and assistance because my father had beaten her and she was running away from him, so she could not return to him."

"Where does your aunt live?"

"There in El Paso. As a matter of fact, my mother got ill after my brother was born. Months later, she left him with my aunt and returned to Mexico seeking medical attention and died."

"Oh, my goodness!" I was horrified. "But why did she leave?"

Roberto looked at me and in a matter-of-fact tone said, "Because she had come to the United States and entered without inspection, she was not admitted, so she was illegally in the United States. She could not return to the hospital where she had given birth, because they had admitted her as an emergency. She had no health insurance, no money to pay for medical services, and she was afraid she would be caught and deported with her son."

"But she did leave!" I pointed out.

Roberto agreed, "Yes, I know, but she went directly to her older brother's home, and they took her to the hospital, which was in another town, and my father never knew anything until she died, and he found out then that she had died and had left her baby in the U.S.,"

"And what happened then?" I asked.

"He was angry and managed to cut across the U.S. without being caught, and grabbed the baby from my aunt and brought him back to Mexico with him."

"So how did Rafael return? When did he return?"

I could tell this was beginning to tire Roberto out. "Well, my aunt had protected him and had gotten his birth certificate and managed to have him baptized before my mom had left, so there were documents stating he had been in the States and born in the States. When we all crossed illegally years ago, he came with us, and it was not until we were here that we found out he was an American!"

"How did you find out?"

Roberto laughed and leaned into the desk. "When we first came to the United States, we looked for our aunt. She had been my mother's older sister, and they had been very close. She was the first one we wanted to see and ask for help. That is when she gave Rafael his papers and told him he was safe here because he had been born here, at a hospital."

With that, I thanked Roberto for coming and being so open and informative. I told him we would continue the process to bring back Gabriela.

Again, I was amazed. Unlike the newspaper reports, Rafael was a citizen, and we had to help Gabriela return quickly. I asked Ann to help me, and between the two of us, we wrote letters to different agencies to obtain the appropriate documents. I called the aunt and found her not too willing to help. Because of the news articles, she was afraid this might affect her status in the U.S., but she was a citizen, and I told her she had nothing to fear. We found out the name of the priest who had baptized Rafael and got a statement from him. The other documents that were valuable were his early vaccines taken right after birth. We quickly assembled all the documents and sent them to The Consulate in El Paso, Texas, to the Fraud Office. And we waited....

Months passed. Rafael came to see us frequently, and I asked him to send for his passport. With the documents I had gotten together and the passport he was able to obtain, we mailed them to The Consulate. They had not acknowledged receipt of the documents or what they considered. We had heard nothing.

Then one day, Rafael called, all excited. "Señora Diana, she is coming back!"

"What?" I was so happy. "What happened? We still have not heard anything from The Consulate. "

"Yes, she received a call from The Consulate telling her she had to make an appointment to hand over her passport and she would be given her residence visa."

"Do not worry, Rafael, we will do that and have Jose Luis, our agent down at the border look after her. How is she doing?"

I could hear it in his voice that he was all choked up. "It has been hard. Little Geovanni cries all the time. The older kids help, but it has been hard."

I stared at the phone, "Yes, I can only guess how difficult it has been for all of you. Thank God, she finally got approved!"

"Yes, *Señora* Diana, and thank you so much for all your help. You and your staff have been great. All the letters, the documents you assembled and managed to send to them, and make them see that I was legitimate, we cannot thank you enough."

"Thank you, Rafael, it is our job. But I am glad we succeeded. "

After I hung up, I couldn't help but throw my arms up in triumph. "YES!" We had won. One more victory in the long battle for immigration justice! One more family on the verge of reuniting!

I had known for a long time that this was my calling—to help people reunite with their loved ones and build a better future together. They were immigrants, but so were we, if not at one point in our lives, then at one point in history. This was simply the latest wave. And just as generations before them—English, Scots, French, Italians, Germans, Asians—they too would find their place in this country. They would settle, grow, raise children, and in time, they would lay claim to their own piece of the United States, shaping its future as so many had before, and it all began with The Statue of Liberty. The phrase rang in my head, "Give me your tired, your poor, Your huddled masses yearning to breathe free, The wretched refuse of your teeming shore. Send these, the homeless, tempest-tost to me, I lift my lamp beside the golden door!"[2]

---

[2] "The New Colossus," a sonnet inscribed on a bronze plaque attached to the pedestal of the State of Liberty.

Chapter 9

JUANITA

Gabriela had returned, carrying little Geovanni with her. He was a year older than I remembered him and was practically running. I noticed Gabriela had a certain fortitude, the way she carried herself, more self-assured. I was happy to see her. Spending a year away from the family had obviously taught her self-reliance and independence. But she had suffered, and there was something in her eyes; the lights had turned off, or the light I once noticed had disappeared.

I did not want to pry, so I did not ask much. I was delighted to see her. Father Paul walked in and gave her a hug, and we sat around and chatted. I took her passport and entered her visa number into our computer.

I was requesting Gabriela's Green Card. Since she was in the country with her residence visa, she had a year to purchase her Green Card, to the tune of $220, to obtain her credential that would prove her Permanent Legal Resident status, allowing her to drive and live legally in the United States.

Once she left, Father Paul turned to me and said, "Do you have a minute? I need to talk to you."

I sat down, "Sure, Father. What is up?" He had a sad look in his eyes, and I felt uncomfortable.

"You know, Diana, we have come a long way." And he looked at me intently. "You have come a long way. Look at all the families that you and everyone here in the office have helped. It is truly remarkable. I am so thankful that God put you in our path. Our Ministry has grown rapidly, and there will be changes as we go along."

I noticed he was leading to something. "Yes." I agreed.

"Well, you know that our Franciscan according to the Catholic Church system allows priests to live in one stable community for some years, and then, we have to move somewhere else."

I felt my heart stop. "You are leaving, Father?"

Once again, he looked at me intently. And softly, he answered, "Yes, I have been ordered to move to Arizona."

"Oh no!" It was an honest reaction. "Oh Father, I know they move you around, but you cannot leave. We have so much to do still and…."

"Diana," he cut me off softly. "I must obey. I have been here for more than nine years. That is unusual for our traditions. Usually, we go every two years. And I leave the Ministry in good hands. You, Mercy, Ann, and they will appoint another priest to take over. Nothing much will change."

I looked at him. *Nothing much would change.* Was he kidding? Not having Father Paul around to seek counsel, to be such a part of the community. He had been the heart of our community, the leader who led softly and firmly, with a big heart and a sound mind. Always careful not to hurt anyone's feelings, understanding the cultural differences between all, respecting them, and seeking justice for all. He had been such a voice of justice in our community and in the town. Bringing healing at their times of grief. Standing up for them when he needed to and going off to marches and demonstrations, always teasing me because I did not. Not having Father Paul around was going to be hard, if not impossible. I knew I was going to really miss him.

But I knew that we had to be strong and make the best of the change. By June of 2009, he had been gone, and then, another would come in his place. I only prayed that the new priest would be as understanding as Father Paul had been.

We prepared for Father Paul's going-away party. It took weeks to put together, and on the day of the celebration, the community came together and expressed their love for him and their gratitude. There was a mariachi band singing, dance groups, tasty food, and even a video of the beginning our Ministry. We knew that a chapter in our lives was ending, and that the new chapter had many questions and fears of what lay ahead for all of us.

Our law office was expanding into new areas. After Father Paul's departure, we incorporated additional programs into our legal services. We began assisting applicants with work permits, including Central Americans with Temporary Protected Status (TPS), and handling more Adjustment of Status cases. These cases involved individuals who had arrived with visas, remained in the U.S., and, through marriage or family sponsorship, could secure legal residency. Unlike the consular process, which required applicants to leave the country, these individuals could complete their legal proceedings while remaining in the United States. Additionally, since the law permitted travel in certain cases, we also learned how to apply for travel permits—commonly known as Advance Paroles.

Ann and I had become highly efficient in our consultations, enabling us to assist more people, which in turn, fueled the growth of our office. As demand increased, we hired a team of interpreters to support clients at local courts for traffic citations, at medical appointments, and during immigration proceedings. Ann's scholarly approach to immigration law ensured we adhered to legal guidelines with precision. She became my go-to resource whenever I needed clarification, always referring to our extensive collection of law books.

Those law books were a treasured asset, purchased through a generous grant from a law firm in Atlanta that had learned about our work through CLINIC. I was overwhelmed when we received the thousand-dollar check—especially from a firm that actively practiced immigration law in the city. It was deeply gratifying to know that our work as Accredited Representatives, authorized by the Department of Justice despite not being lawyers, was recognized and valued by others in the legal community.

Ann's graciousness was admirable. Together, she and her husband, Bill, had made inroads into our Latino community and often invited couples and families over for dinners at their home. She and her husband loved to cook, and they were great at it. They were prime examples of loving Americans who took in our new Latino neighbors. I had visited the couple at their country home, and they had a few acres that they had planted together. Retired from their previous endeavors, they were busy looking after grandchildren, traveling, and when she was with us, Bill assisted part-time at an accounting firm. They were a retired couple, yet still active and thriving.

Juanita Perez entered my life in the midst of change and uncertainty.

The Immigration Reform Bill of 2007 had only raised our hopes, and then it was dashed when House Speaker John Banner shelved it and let it gather dust. The majority in Congress, the Republicans, had seen to it, to block anything on immigration, even if the bill had been signed in bipartisan fashion. But Banner was paying attention to his Right-Wing Caucus, and nothing happened.

From then to 2009, nothing much had happened. President Obama became highly criticized by the Latino community for forcing so many deportations. We knew that the order was to deport all criminals or individuals with high incidents of crime or DUIs. However, ICE was indiscriminate. They went around, forcing themselves into an apartment and detaining and eventually deporting men regardless of whether or not they had a criminal background.

After Father Paul left, there was a great deal of ill will within two small cities. The one we lived in, the Chief of Police, had promised not to detain or arrest for no cause, or because of people's immigration status. The other town, however, had no such policy, and it was the Sheriff's office that delighted in stopping or profiling (which is illegal) and detaining people and placing a detention hold on them immediately.

It was at the height of this that Juanita came to my office carrying a large Kroger plastic bag that was bulging. She was barely four feet tall, and sat in a chair with her feet dangling like a small child. She had a long braid on her back.

"I want to know if you can finish my case."

I smiled and reassured her that I would try, but she had to describe, from the beginning to the end, what her case entailed.

At that, Juanita crossed her hands and placed the bag on another chair. "Well, I came to the United States, following my husband back in 2000. He had gotten sick and told our oldest to send for me so I could come take care of him. I came with a group without being stopped at the border. My husband was already a legal permanent resident, but he needed help and wanted me to be with him, and after that, he got well enough to work. I left everything behind, my animals and home, just to follow him."

"You were not detected when you crossed?"

"Nah, the coyote he hired was good. We hid during the night and then crossed in the dark, and managed to keep walking for hours until we came to a ravine and rested. We slept there."

"Were you alone?"

"Nah, I was with our smallest children. We have four sons. Two had already come with him before."

"Oh, my goodness, how old were they?" I was amazed that they would endanger children in this crossing.

"Well, back then, Manuel was 3, Miguel was 5, Samuel was 7, and Rafael was 9 years old."

"And you were not caught?"

"Nah," She smiled proudly. "After the crossing, the contracted guide (the coyote) took us to the house where we stayed for days until my husband came for us and we traveled to Kentucky."

"So, I am to believe that somehow, sometime, your husband applied for all of you?"

She smiled again, "Yes, but nothing has happened."

"What do you mean?" and I waved at her bag and said, "Do you have papers I can see?"

She stepped from her chair and opened the bag. Out poured dollar bills and documents. I laughed, "Oh my, you have it all!!"

"Well," she said, "I do not know how much it will cost, but I am tired of waiting and want to finish this." As she took out papers, she handed them to me.

I started sifting through the documents and found the birth certificates of everyone and Juanita's marriage certificate. Included in the bunch of papers were the receipt notices and their case numbers, which would make it easy to find them in the system.

After looking at them, I said, "Well, it seems that your husband applied a few years after obtaining his residency, around 1997." I turned to my computer and searched for the Visa Bulletin, which is the schedule of visas coming out from immigration that determines, based on your category, what applications they are looking at and adjudicating.

I turned to her, "Unfortunately, Juanita, they are barely looking at applications that arrived in 1993, so we still have a few years to wait."

She looked at me, not really understanding what I was saying. All she heard was that she had to wait more years. She sighed, got down from her chair, and opened the bag further. She gathered all the dollar bills in her hand and turned and deposited them on my desk. "Here, this is all I have. I hope this is enough to do my case."

I looked at them, a bit amused, but knowing this was serious and had cost this woman many hours of hard labor, I began to count the bills and found she had brought $900.00.

"Yes, of course, this will be enough to finish your case, Juanita. But, let me give you a receipt, you have to sign my entrance in your case as your Accredited Representative, and then, I will explain something to you, before you leave."

She returned to her seat and again smiled and said, "Whatever you need, whatever you can do, I am grateful."

I filed out a G-28, Entrance of New Attorney or Accredited Representative, and had her sign it. I told her she had to take another G-28 to her husband and have him sign it. She looked down and was noticeably quiet.

"What is the matter?"

"Well, my husband does not stay here long. He now goes back to Mexico and lives with his other family."

"What do you mean?"

"Yes," Her eyes welled up with tears. "He left us some time ago and told me he was leaving and would return whenever. My son, Rafael, found out he had another woman and had kids with her, and that is why he came to us only now and then."

Immediately, my heart sank. I knew this was going to be a problem. Somehow, we would have to keep her husband involved in their cases and did not know how that was going to go, even if he had applied for all, he had another family interest. At least, he had not asked her for a divorce.

"Is your relationship still good with him?" I asked.

She looked at me sternly before replying, "I should beat him up." She then softened her tone. "But I know we have to keep him happy, or he pulls his support from us."

"Look, Juanita, I am sorry for that. And please understand that I do not want to get involved in your marriage. But, if you want this to go forward, you must keep your husband happy and involved in this, or else, you will not become a resident and you have already lived here since 2000 so you have been here ten years, since it is 2010 now, and we do not know how much longer immigration is going to take to process your case."

She was not happy, and her look was that of resignation, her head slightly tilted downward, her eyes to the ground, and her hands crossed at her lap.

"If the system is working with applications from 1993, and though I know that four years does not seem like much, you must understand that this system goes up and down.

The government has quotas." She raised her head and looked at me quizzically. I knew she did not understand.

"That they have issued a set number of visas to give per year. For instance, for the 1st Category, which is for family members of citizens, the amount is 200,000 worldwide. That means all over the world that applied, only 200,000 visas. Not much. And they process those that arrived in January, and they wait another few months before they process those that arrived in February. So, you cannot figure out by years, but by months and years, and it practically doubles the time."

She understood, "What you are saying then is that I have a long wait."

I moved my head in agreement, "Yes."

She sat quietly, and I figured she was wondering how she would continue her relationship with a husband who no longer loved her. I felt very bad for her. Immediately, this small woman had touched my heart. She was alone, but for her sons' sake, she kept fighting to survive.

"Juanita, what do you do for a living?"

She brightened up. "I make tamales. I go from house to house taking orders. On Friday, I go buy the materials and begin cooking until late, and then on Saturday, I go out and deliver. Would you like some?"

I laughed, "Of course I would! Tell you what, you make me a dozen, half red and half green, and I will pick them up on Saturday afternoon, ok?"

She stood up and came around for me to give her a hug goodbye. "How spicy?"

"Not too spicy, Juanita. I am not a good Mexican; I do not like spicy food."

Her eyes widened, "NO?" *How could that be? ALL Mexicans ate hot food.*

"No, my mother was American, and we did not eat spicy food at home."

She smiled, "Oh, that's why." It made sense now. It was like I was now forgiven. It is sacrilegious to be around Mexicans and not eat hot spicy foods. Those who worked around me and knew me were aware of this and did not make a big deal about it. It was a given that Diana did not eat spicy food. Do not give her any jalapeños or habaneros or whatever. My brothers had married Mexican women and were used to the hot spicy foods. When I visited them, the food would not have the spicy ingredients for my sake, and everyone had the hot spicy salsas on the side. I appreciated their consideration.

When I got home that night, I sat down and opened my diary. It had been days since I had written in it:

Since I began working in the Hispanic Ministry, people have come into my life and made me a better person. They are mostly humble, from poor stricken towns where food is scarce, work is scarce, and life is precarious. How lucky we are in this country to have everything we need. After every trip back from Latin America when I was working as a consultant, I saw so much poverty and such hunger that it would make me angry to see my own grandchildren be fussy and not eat their food. I did not do the "children in China narrative" to make them eat, but it would make me angry to see food thrown. I still remember the children lined up before their first morning class, waiting with bowls that would be filled with chicken soup, and they had large glasses filled with milk. That would be their only meal for the day. And they were eating that because of the work of the Agency for International Development, USAID, and our project, or another country's project, was pouring millions of dollars into seeing that children got fed, that children had the opportunity to learn. During my time in El Salvador, where I spent more time than any other country because it was at war, the many governments with projects were astounding. The GTZ from Germany, UNICEF, the French group, the Spanish group, and the Italian and Canadian Agency for Development, to name a few. Amazingly, we did not do the same things, and the Salvadorans, in those years, were able to receive the best teacher training, curriculum development, and issuance of textbooks and libraries, of which I was a part, that any other time in their history. I have often wondered what would have happened if, after the war, our consulate, our office would have listened to us and really tried to establish a post-traumatic stress training nationwide for a country so touched by war and so weakened in their human development. War does horrible things to people, it dehumanizes some. At the time, they told us they did not have any money. It was also not on the political agenda of our government. Before I left, Salvador for the last time, I had learned of how, after the peace had been signed, bandits or roaming gangs had gotten hold of weapons left by our soldiers. I was also saddened by the news that President Clinton was deporting all the Salvadoran gangs back to El Salvador. And the people were frightened. The mayors we had trained, and city leaders were concerned that they were not equipped to deal with this onslaught of unsavory returnees. But it had been politically expedient for us, and the Salvadorans were now going to suffer a new war, the war of drugs and savage crime. Without knowing then, we were creating a new chapter with Central America that would come back to bite us.

Chapter 10

TOMAS

I seldom took vacations, and in the beginning of 2010, I went to Mexico to visit my family. Though I had made my life in the States, my family had not. They all lived in Mexico, had thriving families and businesses. One of my brothers owned an import business, and the other had a real estate company. They had no desire to live in the United States and had no reason to, really. They traveled a great deal, and we would often see each other in unusual places or countries.

It was during one of my visits with my family that I received a frantic phone call from Ann.

"Diana, you have to hurry back!"

"Why? What happened?"

"Remember that young man, Tomas, for whom you did the Adjustment of Status a couple of months ago? His mother had just obtained her residency, and his father was a permanent resident?"

"Yes, what is new?"

"Well, Tomas came by this morning, excited and scared. He got a letter called Notice to Appear, and he has a court date?"

"A court date?"

"Yes, he is scared they are going to deport him!!"

"Deport him? Oh goodness, no!" I was alarmed. Had I known then what I know now, I would have told Ann not to worry, that the court date would take time, and we could see Matt and ask him to help us. But I did not know, and at that time, it scared me to death thinking that I had done something wrong, that I was not meticulous enough.

"When is his court date?"

"Next month," Ann answered.

"Ok Ann, I am going to try to leave on Friday. Try setting an appointment with Matt. We need him on this one. I will see you next Monday. Thanks so much for letting me know."

Tomas Salinas was a tall, slender young man—lean and wiry, standing over six feet. His jet-black hair framed a striking face, with dark eyes that held an undeniable charm. He bore a resemblance to the actor Orlando Bloom, though taller, with curlier hair and a less broad-shouldered build. Gualdemiro had recommended him to me, and naturally, I was eager to help.

His father, a legal resident, had petitioned for Tomas, his sisters, and their mother. However, complications arose with his mother's application after his father fell victim to a Notario—an unscrupulous fraudster posing as an immigration specialist. Notarios exploit vulnerable individuals, falsely claiming expertise while filling out legal documents without understanding—or caring about—their clients' immigration history. They take money under the guise of "helping," yet more often than not, they leave families entangled in disastrous legal trouble. Opportunists. Swindlers. Tomas and his family had paid the price.

In the early 2000s, the backlog of family applications for legal residents was staggering. Most families faced wait times of 10 to 15 years before receiving approval to reunite legally in the U.S. If a legal resident had applied for their family in 1992, their application wouldn't progress until 2006—meaning a grueling 14-year wait before their loved ones could finally enter the country.

Many legal residents had obtained permanent status by 1990, so if they submitted applications in 1992, any teenage child included in the petition often faced an unfortunate reality: by the time their case was reviewed and adjudicated, they had "aged out." In other words, once a child turned 21, they no longer qualified to immigrate under their parents' application and had to start the process all over again, falling into a different family-based immigration category—one that carried an even longer wait time.

Tomas was on the verge of falling into this category, making his mother's application critically urgent. We needed to accelerate the process. Fortunately, once his mother obtained legal residency, we could submit Tomas's application under the 245i law, which allowed him to apply for legal status while already inside the United States. He paid a $1,000 fine for entering without admission, but at the least, this provided a pathway for him to remain with his family.

As soon as I returned that Monday, I called Matt's office and made an appointment to see him. Matt's office, the Office of Immigration at Catholic Charities of Louisville, Kentucky, had several legal secretaries as well as paralegals and a few other lawyers. We had framed our price schedule a bit below theirs to maintain our motto of helping the underserved and underprivileged immigrants. Both Tomas and I entered Matt's office, worried about what was to come. As usual, Matt came up to me and gave me a quick hug, and we sat down.

His keen, blue eyes began reading the papers we handed him, and he asked us for the rest of Tomas' file, which was not much because Notarios[3] are notorious con artists who do not keep track of documents, even the originals. What we had seemed to be enough for Matt to make a quick appraisal of the problem.

"Well, it is not as bad as it looks." He sat at his desk in front of us. "What we have here is the possibility of applying for Tomas' residency based on his mother's application." Then he turned to Tomas and said, "Has your mother entered the U.S. with her residency?" I turned to Tomas and interpreted what Matt had asked.

Tomas shook his head. He was a bit nervous. "No, todavía, no." (No, not yet.)

Matt turned to me. "Diana, she must come immediately. We are running against time. Once she is in and we have her green card, we can proceed. What I will do is have Tomas

---

3   *Notarios are fraudsters who con people into believing they are immigration specialist, and they are not.*

go alone to Chicago without me or any lawyer at his Master Hearing."

I turned and interpreted to Tomas what Matt had explained. Tomas looked at me, startled. Seeing that, Matt put his hand out as if to stop his worry, "It is your first court hearing, you do not need a lawyer. You will have to wait all day to be seen, but in the end, the judge will give you another court date. And that is what we want, *time*."

Again, I turned to Tomas and interpreted. This had not made Tomas any less nervous; he looked at me and in Spanish said, "And what about ICE? Won't they arrest me and deport me?"

I asked Matt regarding Tomas's concern, and he smiled, "NO, tell him that ICE does not appear in court, at least not in Chicago. There will be no law enforcer. Only judges, lawyers, and people. He has nothing to worry about."

Once I relayed that to Tomas, he seemed to relax. Matt had returned to the documents, and then he said, "You know? When he is there, he can ask for a Change of Venue. He can ask the judge to change his court to here, and I will take it from there."

Tomas looked at me, not understanding, and I told him I would explain later what that meant. I thanked Matt profusely, knowing how skilled he was and believing that this was going to have a good ending.

As we left Matt's office, I explained the significance of a change of venue—how it would buy us the time needed for Tomas' mother to enter the country, secure her green card, and establish her presence before we proceeded further. What I didn't share with Tomas, however, was what Matt had explained to me: there was a strong legal argument that could make Tomas an exception to the usual rule. Matt was confident, knowing that many judges were unfamiliar with this particular legal nuance. He saw an opportunity to test the theory and potentially have Tomas's case approved.

It was a calculated risk—not because Tomas didn't deserve the exception, but because a judge might reject the argument outright, ruling against him and ordering his deportation. Yet this was precisely why I admired Matt. He wasn't just a lawyer; he was a strategist willing to push boundaries for his clients, armed with deep knowledge of the law and an unshakable commitment to using it in their favor. In all the time I had known him, Matt had never failed. His track record gave me confidence, but I kept my concerns to myself—Tomas was the type to worry incessantly, and there was no reason to burden him with fear so early in the case.

I did not see Tomas for many months after that, when I found out that his mother had entered the States and that he had returned to Matt, and his case had moved forward. He came into my office one afternoon and asked me if I could interpret for him at Matt's office. It turned out it was not at Matt's office but in the immigration building, where they did teleconferences with the judge in Memphis. We greeted each other and passed through security, and Matt told me he wanted me to go in with him. I was explaining that I could not since I was not a lawyer, and he grinned and said, "Just follow me." Then the immigration officer motioned us inside with Matt, Tomas, and me following suit.

We stepped into a small room furnished with two tables, a large TV screen looming in front of us. Tomas sat at the far end of the left table, Matt in the middle, and I at the other end. On the screen, the judge and immigration prosecutor appeared, ready to proceed.

Matt introduced himself, answering the judge's initial questions with ease. I sat still, bracing for the moment when the judge might ask who I was—but that question never came.

Then, Matt retrieved the case documents, thick and carefully bound, and launched into his argument. The prosecutor quickly interjected, attempting to shut down Matt's reasoning. But the judge listened carefully, weighing every word before ruling for a continuance, giving himself time to study Matt's argument and the legal framework surrounding the case.

As we walked out, silence hung between us. Only when we reached the bottom floor, far from the ears of any immigration officers, did we exhale. Tomas looked unsettled—confused and anxious, uncertainty clouding his face.

Matt was a little excited, and he smiled broadly, "What just happened is exactly what I wanted to happen. I provided the judge with ample case law to justify my petition and argument, and he did not know it, so rather than rule without knowing it, he has given himself time to read it and will rule against any objections that the prosecutor will have."

I turned and interpreted to Tomas. "Will this mean that I will lose the case?" He was troubled and asked, wide-eyed. I turned to Matt and explained.

Matt shook his head. "No, this is a good thing. Because this exception to the law is not used often, most judges do not know it. And in order not to appear too ignorant before us, I could guess that he would rule in our favor because I had shown him precedents."

After relaying to Tomas, I could see Tomas relax. We had walked across the expanse of the federal building, and we were out in the street. We shook hands, and Tomas and I walked to my car.

"*No te preocupes, Tomas,*" (Don't worry, Tomas,) I laughed, "*¡Tenemos el mejor abogado de la ciudad!*" (We have the best lawyer in town!)

I sent Tomas back to his jobsite, and I returned to the office and relayed the entire incident to Ann, who laughed and rejoiced along with me with regard to the skill and amazing knowledge of the law that Matt had. We were so lucky to have him in our corner.

The days that followed that incident engulfed us in the preparation for the new priest who had been assigned to our Ministry as the new coordinator. He was being sent from another state and originally was from Jalisco, Mexico. Father Jose Bautista was to arrive soon, and the Dean of our Deanery was going to bring him over to introduce him to us. I was not concerned since I felt that he would be someone we could work with, and things would not change much.

I was soon to find out that would not be the case.

Dear Diary,

I write in true consternation. I must vent somewhere, and you are the one I can talk to about this. The new priest is a prima donna. Forgive me for saying that, he is being a holy man and all that. Though I do not know how holy he is, such a change from Father Paul. I was really ticked off at how he has come in and expected us to do things we are not used to doing. Unlike Father Paul, who let me run our office with hardly any intrusion, this man wants to know what we are doing, where we are going, etc. Really aggravating. What really bothers me the most is that he charges for everything. And that is not right. But I have no one to go to and people are complaining. If he does not get involved in our charges and begins to tell me we must charge more, everything will be ok. Besides, if he does, I will show him that one reason we can become accredited is because we follow the guidelines of charging less than the Department of Justice requires. We are SERVING the people! I wonder if he ever heard of that?? Yesterday, he and Mercy had words; she does not mince words at all, and she did not agree with what he was asking for in the Confirmation preparation. Frankly, I do not know but would guess that Mercy is right. I worry about her because she really loses her temper, and I am afraid she is not going to want to stay long. I would hate to have her go too. We have worked so well all these years, why did this man have to come and shake everything up so?

After many of the changes that the new priest brought about, we began to hear that the archdiocese was thinking of closing the school across from us, the Catholic School. Many of our community children had been assisting and now we had to worry if the school closed, where were they going to go? It really was not our concern, because we had become a legal office and did not get involved with church things. But Father Jose made it our concern.

"Diana, you must find a new space for these children in other schools, Catholic schools."

"Forgive me, Father, but would that not be the work of the principal, the parents and school organizations? To help parents find a place for their kids in educational institutions. I know nothing about Catholic schools or the people who run them."

He was a stocky man, built like a bull and as bull-headed as one. He pushed aside my concerns, "No, *Señora* Diana, we must find places for these kids and soon. You work with the city officers and know about new legislation; there is something there we can use for the kids."

I had heard of a new program that the State was launching. They were vouchers that parents could use to send their kids to private schools if they did not want them in public schools. I was not in favor of the proposition because I felt that our public schools were fine. However, as days passed, and parents became more alarmed as to the academic future of their children, they started calling our office to seek assistance in the matter.

I asked Mercy for help, and between the two of us, we were able to talk to two schools, Catholic schools nearby, that could accept these children into their schools with the vouchers and an additional charge. Father Paul had won several grants for our children's education, and from those funds, had paid for their education in the school that was being closed. I knew this priest had no intention of writing grant proposals. Unlike the smooth path we had with Father Paul, our road was now rocky and full of obstacles.

In those transition months, the only joy we were able to get was from the different cases that we were able to win, and then Tomas walked into the office one day, showing me his green card.

"¡Oh Tomas, que alegría!" (What a joy!)

He smiled broadly, "Sí, Matt es un excelente abogado. El juez decidió en mi favor y la semana pasada me llego por correo." (Yes, Matt is a fine lawyer. The judge ruled in my favor, and last week I got this in the mail!)

"Muy bien, ve y dale las gracias a Matt. ¿Y por cierto, ahora qué vas a hacer?" (Great, well go and thank Matt, and what are you going to do now?)

He sat down and looked at me shyly. "¡Diana, voy a regresar a la escuela!" (I am going back to school!)

"Que?" (What?) I almost jumped. "¡Eso es fantástico! ¿Dónde vas a estudiar?" (That is great! Where and what are you going to learn?)

He laughed, then, in Spanish, he replied, "Well, first I must learn good English, then I want to start my GED and finish if possible. After I got my legal papers, I had thought of going into some sort of business, but then decided not to. I had been approached by some people, and then decided it was all a swindle and changed my mind. I want to get ahead and make something of myself, in return for all the demanding work my dad did to bring all of us here. It is my turn to work hard and succeed."

"Oh, Tomas," I was overjoyed. "That is great. I so wanted to see you move forward, to move ahead. You are just the type of person to succeed. I know you will do great. If you need anything, see me," I said.

With that, he got up and hugged me. "Don't worry, I will." I was impressed by his warmth, eagerness, and happiness. For now, he knew what he was doing and where he was going. I wish I had met more like him to motivate.

It would take a few years, but eventually, we did have many young people come into our office to motivate toward success. Firstly, we had to live through the closing of the local school and the placement of students in other schools, which we were able to do. Then, we had to put up with Father Jose, who failed us repeatedly with his manner, his sermons, and his attitude towards service. I would often ask God why this man was a priest and why he was ordained. But we managed with the utmost toleration, and somehow, the days passed, and we continued to grow.

And then, instead of hearing all the dreadful things that President Obama was doing to the Latino community or immigrants at large, including all the detainers and deportations, we began to get excited about a new program he was thinking of starting. It was called "Deferred Action for Childhood Arrivals," otherwise known as DACA.

Upon learning of this immigration policy, I turned to Ann and said, "DACA is going to change the lives of hundreds of young immigrants."

Ann replied, "Yes, remember how disappointed we had been with the Immigration Reform that was placed on hold in 2007? Quite frankly, I did not believe much would be accomplished with that."

"Well," I continued. "We had seen how those who opposed the President would stop at any cost to keep him from achieving anything that smacked of favoring our cause. And DACA now is going to be big, noticeably big."

Ann scoffed. "I am sure by the time all the hoopla has passed and gone, we are going to see challenges."

I knew she was right, but at that moment, I needed people, lots of people, and all I had were Mercy and Ann. Knowing I was not going to count much on Father Jose, I immediately made phone calls and publicly asked for volunteers who were residents or citizens. And I programmed a seminar, out in the church auditorium.

The group of young people that showed up was a good number. About fifteen people wanted to help. I went through the program with them. I told them I needed them to set up a workshop where people would come and sign up and answer a few key questions. Consequently, each received a sheet of paper with the requirements and costs of the program, and then, the people would call in to make appointments, and the processing would begin.

The first workshop we did, we had about 150 young people show up. From there onward, it was word of mouth. Once I had gotten the information across, I needed to hire people who could assist with sign-up and gathering information, as well as sharing relevant information with those who signed up. Then I remembered Tomas. I called Tomas, and he had finished his GED. He was looking for work and was eager to work with us. Little did I know that this was to be a fateful event. Having Tomas come to work with us would change our office from a one-person act to a team.

Chapter 11

SERIOUS TRAINING AND THE FUN BEGINS

The next day, I came to work, and there was a young, sophisticated, dapper man waiting for me. It was Tomas, dressed in a light blue shirt, paired with a silk tie and a pair of polished, black shoes. I almost mistook him for a lawyer. His good looks were accentuated by his smile and his friendly disposition. I could tell he was nervous about his first day. I could not help but smile as I ushered him into my office. He sat down and looked intently at me.

"Bueno Tomas, this is an important day. We are starting on a big program that will affect millions of young people." He looked serious, and his eyes widened. "What do you want me to do?"

I sat across from the desk from where he was sitting. "I am going to teach you how this program works. Then, I am going to ask for volunteers to come help us, and I want you to teach them, and we need to have a smooth operation to process so many people."

"Of course, I understand, but I do not know anything about immigration."

"Yes, I know. That is why I will teach you, and little by little, you will gain enough experience to begin seeing clients on your own."

Hiring Tomas to join our organization felt truly providential. From the start, I trained him on the fly, juggling a mountain of urgent tasks. Fortunately, Tomas was remarkably adept—a quick learner who absorbed everything at an impressive pace. I was impressed at his language learning. He spoke English well and easily conversed. Before long, I could entrust him with handling all new DACA cases, which proved to be a game-changer for all of us in the office. Tomas's natural ability to connect with young applicants, gather their information, and guide them through the process was invaluable.

Ann also pitched in, and we managed to bring in volunteers, but it was Tomas who quickly took charge. DACA wasn't just a lifeline for young people who had grown up here—it was a gateway to the American Dream. For our office, it also became a crucial source of stability and growth. What I hadn't realized at first was just how essential this program would be. Time and again, when our funds ran low, DACA candidates reached out, bringing in much-needed financial support that kept us afloat. It was nothing short of a blessing.

Our relationship with the head office at the church had never been great. I had always felt that they put up with us because the parish priest allowed us to do what we did without any intrusion. But there had always been ill will since we were Latinos and not white. This church was primarily white Irish German, and our brown skin and our language grated their sensibilities, especially to the older ladies that serviced the church. I had several run-ins with the main secretary and had complained to Father Paul, and he, as diplomatic as usual, was able to assuage feelings, and things kept moving smoothly. With Father Jose, it was different. He wooed the secretaries and volunteers, and it was we, who had to change our attitude. This began to grate on me.

One of my main complaints about Father Jose was that he never fully allowed or gave permission to do something; he merely said he would think about it and never gave a reason behind the disapproval that would follow. This caused confusion and uproar. He was lucky if someone forgot about their initial request. I had asked him a year after he had arrived, to see from the Parish Priest if we could have our front steps worked on. Otherwise, I thought of utilizing our donations to fund the work.

"Father, the stairs coming up the front are torn apart and becoming dangerous for small children and the elderly."

"Yes, I will talk to Father Mike and see what he says."

"Father, we will not cost the church any money. We can produce the money, and I can call on volunteers, and we will have it done."

"Oh no, Señora Diana, that would not be right. Our people are poor and cannot also provide us with funds for our structure."

I fully agreed on that but thought it hypocritical that he became worried about our "poor" congregation's donations and never worried about them when he was charging them for something they wanted done from the church or from him, like an extra mass. The parties for fifteen-year-old youth, the so-called *Quinciañeras*, were very costly, or a church wedding on a Saturday instead of a Sunday, for example.

So, I waited and waited, and nothing was done. Every time I asked him if he had talked to Father Mike, Father Jose said, "No, I have been busy but will do so right away."

Again, I would not hear from him. This sort of disappointment became the norm, and I grew weary. What finally made me very mad and put me into action was the day I had a child slip and fall, and the mother came in, berating us and saying she was going to sue us. I called Ann into my office.

"Ann, I cannot take it anymore. Please call Javier and Francisco and ask them to see me with a plan for the stairs. We are going to build it and safeguard our community, and I will take the dissension from the church. If I must leave, so be it."

Ann was not someone to scare, and she too was resolved and totally supported me. That would be two people the church would have to get rid of if this did not meet their approval.

The next day, both men came to my office, and we talked it out. I included Ann, and we resolved to purchase the materials with money from a fundraiser we had done, and they would begin work the weekend coming up. And that is how the front stairs were repaired and finished, and Father Jose never said anything.

It never ceases to amaze me how this priest has been selected and is in our midst with the authority to destroy everything we have built with Father Paul, and the Parish priest does not say anything. I wonder how long we will have to live under this man's authority before we can recover and return to normalcy. God give me strength to endure! I prayed.

Months passed, and then, slowly... one year after another. Our DACA program grew highly successful, and we had picked up more clientele, and there was more need in terms of immigration reform. ICE had caused a few scares and had appeared at the doorsteps of apartments. They whisked off standbys, whether they had "papers" or not. The Obama Administration was set on deporting all criminals. We felt he wanted the reform agreed upon by the Group of Eight in Congress, and to give it strength, deportations were needed so he would not be accused by his opponents as being soft on immigration. That was not a feeling our community had of him. Some of us genuinely believed in him, but these actions made it very hard to defend him and say he was really interested in immigrants. The Latino community was not impressed.

The reality was harsh—anyone living in the vicinity of an ICE operation risked being swept up, corralled, and taken without warning. Later, we would have to fight tirelessly to get them released from detention. What enraged me most was the blatant disregard for the law. ICE personnel would storm apartment complexes, pounding on doors before forcing their way inside—without a valid warrant. Their so-called warrants were meaningless, never reviewed by a judge, nor backed by legitimate cause for entry. Instead, they operated with brute force, seizing those inside and dragging them into the system.

Often, local police in some communities showed more compassion; their approach was far less aggressive than that of sheriffs or immigration officers. But for those targeted by ICE, there was rarely mercy—only fear, chaos, and the struggle to reclaim their freedom.

I once received a frantic call from a young woman who had been pulled over for driving without a license—her baby in tow. The police officer was adamant about taking her to jail. She managed to reach me, desperation in her voice, and I immediately asked the officer to wait. Without hesitation, I rushed out the door, jumped in my car, and drove straight to where they were.

When I arrived, I pleaded with the officer, reasoning with him until he finally agreed to let her go. He allowed her to park the car and come with me instead. I thanked him profusely, wasting no time in getting her and her baby into my car before driving away. Moments like that were rare exceptions, but they did happen—and when they did, they meant everything.

The DACA program took its course, and young men began to think they could enlist in the military service. When the United States invaded Iraq in 2003, some of our young men offered to go to war, and I thought to myself, *Why would they risk their lives when no one cared about Latino immigrants?*

I was especially fond of and worried about two parishioners who belonged to very caring families, and

Serious Training and the Fun Begins

after having become citizens, the two enlisted and were off to war. The families continued their lives as if nothing had happened, but I would talk to the mothers, and they were worried and prayed all the time.

Years later, and with the United States still involved in wars, DACA recipients came to my office wondering if they enlisted, would they obtain their legal residence. I told them, "No," that being DACA did not give them the ability to enter the service because the U.S. Defense would not accept anyone who was not a resident or a citizen. Fortunately, the war fever subsided, and we encouraged many, instead, to stay in school, and we could help them get into college.

It was in the middle of this activity that the DACA Program was succeeding, when I heard the church was thinking of closing our ministry. I had just hired a teacher to teach English as a Second Language with a grant I had obtained from a local casino. As a goodwill gesture to the community, the local casino provided thousands of dollars back into the community. Our evening classes were full of the young Latinos who had left school, had dropped out years ago. They were now registered in the local GED program. They needed to learn English to work at a factory or a better location where a GED was required.

The mere idea of moving seemed ludicrous. I had no one to talk to about it and decided to drive to the next city where the archdiocese officers were and discuss this with whoever had the authority.

My trip to the archdiocese office was not successful. It turned out that our church was in heavy debt to the archdiocese. The archdiocese did not want to continue supporting it, and the ministry was just one more expense. Because our work was not church-related, they felt we could move easily. It made me very mad. I was amazed at the lack of consideration for our social work and the positive impact it has had on the community for ten years! Our Catholic church was known for helping disadvantaged people of the world. But I was not going to argue. I was sick and tired of the church office anyway and really felt this was a suitable time to break away cleanly, without any ill feelings. I bid my adieu and returned with ideas of how to move and where to move.

Social Justice has been the cornerstone of our church, I wrote in my diary that evening. *How can the powers that be of this community say that what we do is not the church's work? If taking care of the immigrant is not the church's work, then what is? How is it that there is a Bishops Organization that constantly fights for immigrants, and that there is a group like CLINIC whose mission is to speak for the underserved? These are all Catholic! We have worked so hard to build our law office, to work and see its fruits with over one thousand families being served throughout these years. We have taken care of over two hundred DACA recipients, and now we have so many more families waiting for their processes. We cannot just simply fold. We cannot call in all these people and return their files and say we are sorry, but we must close. That is not an option. We must find the way.*

When I told Ann about what was happening, she became very worried. She had volunteered because our office was not too far from where she lived. She did not like driving a lot anyway, and driving further away was not something she had anticipated. I knew Ann's worth but could not keep her from leaving if she felt she could no longer help us. She had also developed a chronic illness that had kept her from the office for weeks, and I felt the signs on the wall were that we had to move on.

My only option was to negotiate with the church, talk to Father James, who had replaced Father Jose, and ask for the furniture in the office to come with us. We had no money to buy furniture, and even though much of it had been donated to us, we needed it. Father James was pleasant, and he acquiesced, and then I began to look for a new site and a lawyer to help us draw the Articles of Incorporation, or how to organize as a non-profit.

I called Jim Barnes, an old friend and the President of the organization that Father Paul had helped set up. It had been Father Paul's contention that we needed to bridge the gap between the immigrants and local service providers. So back in 2003, the new organization was born. The Anglo-Latino Center had been a referral organization that comprised of variegated members of the community. There were lawyers, doctors, insurance owners, real estate vendors, bank officers, and university representatives. With Father Paul at the helm, the organization obtained different grants to assist different community liaisons with the Latino community. By the time I approached Jim, the organization was languishing without a real mission.

"Jim, I need your help." I had come to his office, a busy legal firm, and Jim was behind his desk, piled with many files.

He pushed some away, "It is all my immediate cases." He grinned. Jim was a medium-sized, thin blonde. He had a beautiful smile and always made people at ease. He was also one of the best contract lawyers in town.

"So, what's up?"

"The ministry is closing." Before I could finish, he yelped, "What?"

"Yes, it is closing, and I am looking for another place to set up shop. I cannot leave all our families out in the cold."

"What do you mean by 'closing?' And why?"

"Look, I even went to the archdiocese and talked about it. It seems the church owes them a lot of money, and they do not want to carry another structure or something. "

"Oh, for Pete's sake!"

"Yeah, well," I continued. "Anyway, I need to draw up Articles of Incorporation and set up shop somewhere else."

Jim looked at me and frowned. "Not happy to hear this, Diana. Especially when there is so much at stake."

"I am glad you said that, Jim. But the matter of fact is that they are determined to push us out, and we must go. So, I need your help."

Jim stared at me, and then there was a gleam in his eye. "What are you talking about? There is already something set up."

I looked at him, perplexed. "What do you mean?"

He pushed back in his chair and laughed. "Goodness, it is before your eyes! Diana, take the Anglo-Latino Center here and run with it."

I was initially shocked. "Oh, I could not. That is what Father Paul started, and you are President and...."

"And we do not know what to do with it," he interrupted me. "And you do. Besides that, my office has grown, our firm is becoming more involved in litigation, and I simply do not have the time to volunteer to the organization. Diana, it makes sense."

I wondered if this was what I needed to do. It sounded and felt right. Before I could answer, Jim called in his secretary and had her bring all the most recent files of the organization. Then, he turned to me. "Look these over, and you will need to go to the bank and change that account from my name to your name. I will call a meeting of the members, and we will vote on passing the organization to you, and I will make the changes in the Articles of Incorporation."

"All I need to do is find a site?"

He grinned, "Exactly!"

I stood up, my head still reeling with ideas and taking in the suddenness of it all. It seemed as if it was falling in place without a hitch.

"Oh, Jim, thank you. I never imagined..."

He came over to hug me. "Yes, I know. But you will do great. You are perfect for it. You have a worthy cause and good service. All you need now is to fund it."

My heart sank when he said that. That was right, I was now moving from an employee base to self-employment, and it was not going to be easy. As I said goodbye to him and walked out of his office, I got in my car and looked up to the sky, "Well, Lord, you put me here, please help."

Ann did not leave right away; she helped me drive around, looking for a new office space. The rental reality was a bit scary since all offices were asking for more money than we could afford. However, unbeknownst to me, the people of the community we had served learned about what was happening and felt that this was about them too, so they decided to organize a fundraiser without informing us. After weeks of looking and looking, I was called into the church's school cafeteria. There, before me, sat about a hundred people, all smiling, and they showed me to a table where I could sit down. Then, the show began.

There were folk dances, and storytelling played out by some of my previous clients, depicting their coming to the United States and the help they had gotten from us. Most of the roles were funny. I saw myself identified as an overworked grandma looking after her chicks. And then, I noticed everyone in our office was depicted in this play. This was the community's way of thanking us for helping them. After the dancing and role-playing, there was food. One cannot have a Latino gathering without food. And we, Hispanics, love to eat. So, we were served tamales and a plate with meat, rice, and black beans. All delicious. And at the grand finale, one of them, my hardworking new citizen, Marisela, stood up and, on behalf of everyone, gave a speech in which she said, "Thank you" for all our work, and she handed me a check. I was floored; somehow, they had raised $2,000. This would pay for our first month's deposit and rent, wherever we found the site. I was pretty choked up.

"I want to thank you for your largesse and your incredible support. You believed in us, and we know how hard all of you work and have worked to bring your families over. We will continue to fight and advocate for your rights and those who still have no legality here. Let it be known that the Constitution of the United States of America does give anyone here, on our soil, the rights of a human being. And we will fight to see that they are not trampled."

From that moment on, we advertised to have everyone who had a case with us, to come and authorize us, to move their files to our new office; they came in droves.

We finally secured a site in the heart of the community, conveniently within walking distance for many. The building housed four other tenants: a lively dance studio, a professional photography studio, an employment agency, and a bustling pizzeria. With the pizzeria right next to us, giving directions was easy—just tell them to find the pizza, and they'd find us.

By the end of 2014, we had moved in and were bustling with activity. Everything seemed to be falling into place. Around that time, we learned that Father Jose had been reassigned to another city, and a new priest would take over the church—but without the Hispanic Ministry. Somehow, despite our presence being closer to the community, it felt like it didn't matter to them.

While grants didn't flood in, we managed to secure enough to keep us going. English and citizenship classes resumed, now offered morning and evening throughout the week. Our spacious office had a large area in the back, perfect for classes and workshops, allowing us to expand our offerings and better serve those who needed them.

One day, I came into the office and a woman from El Salvador who had been part of the church choir was waiting for me. Her name was Angela Garcia Hernandez. She was middle-aged, short, about five feet tall, and had big, expressive eyes. I asked her to sit down, and she sat down slowly, as if she were sore or in pain.

"Are you alright, Angela?"

"Yes, I am fine, *Señora* Diana, I just had to work really hard last night and late, and I am a bit sore."

"Why are you so tired and sore?

Angela was not one to talk ill of anyone. She sighed, closed her hands, and then looked down.

"When I first came to this country, I entered through Miami, since I was coming from El Salvador. I knew no one and then befriended some people who helped me live with them until I found work. I found work with a Cuban doctor; she and her husband owned a laboratory, and she was gone most of the time. They had three kids. The smallest was a baby, and I became not only the housekeeper, but the nanny as well."

"So, you moved in with them and lived in the house?"

She smiled, "Oh yes, I had my own room, and it was nice too, with a TV, a good armchair, and a soft bed. It was all nice."

"But...?" I looked at her expectantly. "There is something wrong, right?"

Again, Angela did not look at me directly but looked down at the desk. "Yes," she replied softly. "Dr. Adriana is very strict and very difficult to live with."

"How's that?"

"More than anything, she is very demanding. She wants me to do more than is sometimes physically possible, and somehow, I manage."

"Angela, you are enabling her to mistreat you. You must stand your ground."

She laughed softly. "I try to. I told her the other day that I was leaving, and quickly, she went into a rant and tirade of how much I owed her. I finally got so angry, I just walked out."

"Well, that was good. Now she knows she cannot harass and bully you."

Angela looked straight at me and leaned into the desk. "I wanted to talk to you because I am worried about something in my past that can hurt me. I want to become a citizen, but I do not know if it will deport me."

I was startled. *What on earth has that dreadful woman done to Angela?*

"Just tell me what it is, and I can tell you the gravity of the situation," I replied.

"I go once a week to Kroger to get food for the family. I have been doing that for years, and the doctor has given me a credit card that I use to make these purchases. One day, I was in line with my cart full of groceries, and my cell phone rang. It is my son who blurts out that he does not want to continue going to medical school, and he is getting out. I was so shocked, I pushed my cart out of the line, away from people, and went to a corner and talked to him. I yelled, I told him how hard I had worked so many years just to provide for him and his sisters to continue in school. I was upset, I was crying."

"Oh, my goodness, I can just imagine. And what did he say, finally?" I was so moved.

In her exertion and retelling, she had allowed tears to stream down her face, and I handed her a tissue. She took the tissue and blew her nose. Then she took a minute to compose herself and continued her story.

"He finally agreed to continue, and he asked for forgiveness, and I ended my call. But when I turned around, there were two men from the store, telling me to follow them into an office."

"Were they from the store? What did they want?"

"Oh Señora, never in my wildest dreams did I imagine I was going to suffer like I did that afternoon. To begin with, my English is not good, and back then, it was nonexistent. I did not understand that they thought I had tried to leave the store with the groceries. I tried to tell them that it was my son's call that had caused me to leave the line and walk away, and I had not looked where I walked away. I was simply talking to him and being upset."

"What did they do?"

"They ushered me into the office and told me to wait. A half hour later, a police officer came in and told me he was taking me to jail. And I cried because I could not go to jail; I had to return to the doctor's house with the groceries. All I could do was give them the card and say, pay, pay."

I could not imagine how this would have appeared to a group of people from a grocery store unused to dealing with immigrants, thinking the worst, without giving her a moment to try to explain herself, pay, and leave. But no, that would have been too simple. Instead, the police officer took Angela to the Police Station and tried to lock her up, but she insisted on calling someone, and she called her sister. Her sister then got a hold of a lawyer who, in turn, got her out.

"After that whole nightmare, I still had to return to the doctor's house with groceries, so I went somewhere else and bought them with my own money."

"Oh, Angela, not knowing the language is sometimes so hurtful."

"Yes," she cried. "And not only did I have to purchase the groceries elsewhere, but I also had to be able to return to the house as if nothing had happened. I also had to pay the lawyer for taking me out of jail and then, my case before the court. The whole thing cost me around $3,000!"

"Oh, my goodness! How did you manage to raise the money?"

She smiled, for the first time in her whole narration. "I had kept my tax return in a savings account for a rainy day, and that was it."

"Ok, I am beginning to understand. You were charged with shoplifting, right?"

She nodded her head, "Yes, it was a felony."

I thought to myself, "The worst." Then, I looked at her straight in the eyes and tried to reassure her. "Look, bring me your charging papers and whatever your lawyer gave you. I really need to see what they charged you with and what the court disposition was." She looked at me, and I could see she had not understood a thing I just said. "What I mean is that I need to see what the policeman said you had done and what the judge decided to do about your case."

"Ahh, si. I think my lawyer said it was dropped."

"Probably dismissed. Well, at any rate, I need to see those papers to determine what problems you may have with immigration if you apply for citizenship. They are getting tough, and now that there is a new administration, they do not like immigrants and will do anything to see that immigrants do not qualify."

She looked scared. Angela had a characteristic that when she was scared, her voice got low and scratchy. "What could they do to me?"

I reached out across the desk and took her hand. "Do not worry. Let me see those papers, and then we will decide if you should try applying for citizenship or not."

She tried to be reassured, but a tear dropped from her left eye. "Angela, I promise you, I will investigate it, and I am sure you will be all right. Look, you really did not do anything wrong. You did not violate any law or commit any theft. You were emotionally distraught and acted like any mother does in a moment of crisis. For now, let me worry about it, and we will get through this, ok?"

"Ay, Señora, God bless you." She got up from her chair and came over to hug me. I hugged her back, and she walked out of the office.

When I got home that night, I took out my diary and began writing:

I am overwhelmed with the bad luck and all the misunderstandings that happen when someone does not speak the language. What happened to Angela happens many times in many different forms and situations. But in the end, it results in our police force taking the wrong attitude and jailing people innocently. Angela is not the first one I have heard that something like this has happened to them. How many clients have I had who signed papers and documents without knowing what was written in them, later causing them much harm? How many clients have come to us seeking counsel because they were talked into doing something they did not know they could not do or should not do? Most of our clients come from poor neighborhoods, lack much education, and have no real worldliness. The saddest part is when I see that our own people, Latinos, take advantage of our community for their own well-being and either put them in harm's way or simply take advantage of them and rob them or take something from them that is not monetary, but their dignity. That always makes me mad, and I seethe when I see that happen. There are many of our people who must learn. I do not know if I am the one to teach them or if they will have time to learn. At least while I am involved in this, I will do everything I can to help them.

The next time I met with Angela, she showed me the documents, and sure enough, the case had been dismissed. She had been charged with shoplifting, but the lawyer had brought it down to "public nuisance," a C Misdemeanor punishable with $500 or 60 days in jail. She paid the money but did not serve any time in jail. So, we had nothing to worry about. I told her she could apply for her citizenship.

From that moment onward, Angela became a faithful student, came every Saturday, and studied diligently. When she came to my office to practice one-on-one, we practiced her retelling her story and making sure the interviewer understood that she had been shocked by her son's phone call and had never had any intention of stealing the food in her cart.

Thankfully, we were successful. After Angela came out of her interview, she immediately called me crying. I was so afraid she had failed; I could not understand her, and her sister took the phone and said, "Señora Diana, she passed, she passed." Glory be, she had passed, and now she would be a proud new citizen. I was so happy. Each student's success was like my own. It never ceased to amaze me how becoming a United States citizen was so important to them. They were proud that their knowledge of U.S. History and Civics surpassed their coworkers. That always made me laugh. The irony of it all, here they were, proud to be citizens, and the native-born citizens cared less for their own history and always looked down on the immigrants.

What was really uplifting about Angela's story is that after all her trials and tribulations and suffering, at the hands of a dragon lady boss, she came into my office one day so excited that she had to stop and catch her breath.

"Look, look, my son just sent me a copy of his Certificate!!" Her eyes shone and she was smiling widely, "He is a full-fledged Doctor!" I took the document from her hands and read the inscription, which stated that indeed Jorge Ruiz Garcia was a doctor in general health.

"You have to be very proud of him," I replied, returning the document to her. "My goodness, Angela, how you have worked and suffered for this moment. I am so happy for you."

She sat down with her hands crossed over her lap. "Yes, I am proud and happy for my son. Now, I worry that while he works in the hospital, he will not get killed."

I was shocked. "What do you mean, killed?"

"Ay Señora, there is so much crime, so many gangs, all is lawless, and the government cannot control it. Doctors, nurses, and all are in danger because these gangs want them to do miracles when they come into the hospital shot, sometimes beyond any chance of survival. And that is the risk my son is taking because he does not have the money to set up his own office, and he does not have any connections with someone in private practice. So, he must work at the General Hospital in downtown San Salvador."

I remembered well, downtown San Salvador, the scene around the hospital near the square in front of the church had been the scene of a huge massacre by the federal forces and the guerrillas. Hard times, challenging times, and still the country was in another war, one of crime and corruption. I shook my head.

"Well, Angela, let's pray that this time of uncertainty passes and that finally, a new government will take over and clear up the mess."

She stood up to leave. "I just had to tell you the good news."

"And I am honored that you came to tell me. Again, I am so happy for you and your son."

I stood up and walked over to her and hugged her. She walked out of my office, and I sat down thinking.

But my thoughts were interrupted by the phone ringing. It was Santos, he wanted to stop by, and would I help him with some papers? Fortunately, I had no more clients after 4pm because they had cancelled, so I first scolded him for trying to quickly visit as if I were not busy, and then told him to hurry over and see what I could do for him.

Ten minutes later, he was in my office. Tomas had stopped by my office, asking if I would see him because he did not have an appointment.

I looked up and sighed, "Yes, Tomas, let him in."

Santos walked in, all excited. "Señora Diana, I need your help. Please, I am going to lose my house if you do not help me." He pushed a handful of papers onto my desk.

I looked at them; they were documents for the refinancing of his home. They were from his bank, and his bank had sold out to another bank.

"Santos, what is the name of your original bank, the Mortgage company?"

He looked at me, unsure he understood where I was going. "The Bank of America."

"So, if your original bank was the Bank of America, it has now sold out to another bank, the Silver Star Bank. That means that your loan is going to another bank, and if you want to refinance, you need to deal with them, not Bank of America."

"Yes, I cannot afford the payments; they have gone up."

"No, Santos, they do not go up. Maybe your taxes have gone up, and now you have to pay more so that the bank has enough in escrow to pay for them twice a year."

Santos looked at me like a deer that had just hit the headlights. He had no idea what I was saying whatsoever.

"Ok, Santos. How much have you been paying?"

"I pay $820 a month, and it has gone to $1000 a month!"

"Fine. What that means is that in your original payment, part of it went to pay the bank interest for lending you the money, part of it went to put away to pay your taxes yearly, and part of it to pay for the actual loan, the principal. Do you understand?"

He was looking at me intently, and he nodded his head.

"Ok, so the auditor of the city, like the accountant, did a survey and found out that all the houses around your neighborhood have sold for more than what you bought your homes for when you bought them. So now your homes are valued more. When the homes are worth more, they pay the city more taxes. Does that make sense?

He grinned, "Si, of course. That is why my cost has gone up?"

"Well, partially, because also, the banks charge interest for their loans, and since your bank sold your loan to another bank, the interest went up. I do not know."

I figured I would have to look that up, because I really did not know. I was not a real estate broker.

"Si, ok, but I need your help to fill out these papers."

I looked at my watch. Santos always did this, coming in at the last minute and wanting help for something that was going to take longer than a few minutes.

"Look, Santos, I have a meeting to go to, so I will make another appointment with you. This is going to take time, and I do not have time right now."

He stood up, "No, that is fine. Thank you for seeing me. But you will help me, please?"

"Yes, Santos, I will." And with that, I sent him out to Tomas, who would place him on our agenda.

That night, after dinner and before I went to bed, I wrote in my diary:

Santos is in his fifties but is so scared of doing anything new. He knows enough English to get himself understood, but he still relies on me to help him with everything. I guess I have enabled him, only because it is easier to do things for him rather than having to redo what was done wrong in the first place. When he came to do his citizenship, I was worried he would not pass. But he surprised me and put his head where it should be, studied hard, and learned. When he walked into my office with his citizenship certificate, I was proud of him. He had done it, and later, in gratitude, he invited me to a party where he had a calf butchered and cooked Mexican style. It's called "Carnitas", very good meat and wonderful tacos. I was part of the community, joking with them and rejoicing in their achievements. It had been a fun afternoon.

Chapter 12

2016-2018 CONVENING IN WASHINGTON, D.C.

Our move to a site within the community felt truly providential. The office was positioned near the densest Latino population, making it easily accessible. Yet, we weren't surrounded by the usual Latino businesses—no taco stands, bakeries, or neighborhood storefronts. Instead, we were set apart in an area that opened into the town's larger commercial district, giving us a professional presence while still being close enough to serve our community without feeling overcrowded.

We carefully divided the office into two sections, separated by a small hallway. Upon entering the lobby, visitors were greeted by a large desk to the right, while a row of chairs lined the left wall, offering a welcoming space for waiting clients. Behind the receptionist's desk, I hung a striking, colorful painting from a renowned Salvadoran artist, adding warmth and vibrancy to the space.

To the right of the hallway were the immigration offices, and across from them, the tax preparation offices. Tomas had launched his new tax preparation business here, creating a natural crossover between our services. Clients who initially came to see me would later return for tax assistance, and Tomas's clients would discover our immigration services in the process. The arrangement worked seamlessly.

Each day, the lobby was bustling with clients waiting to be seen, and in the back of the office, a classroom was filled with students eager to learn. Our operation had grown into a thriving hub of support and education, serving the community in meaningful ways.

One bright sunny morning, Tomas stood, taking it all in. "Wow, we look pretty good, don't you think?"

"Yes," I replied, "I am glad I listened to you and got out of the area where the church was and moved here, closer to the neighborhood. We are walking distance from many neighborhoods, and I guess we can call ourselves the neighborhood immigrant agency." And I smiled.

"Absolutely," Tomas reiterated. "Now we will get more traffic. You know how our people are, once they know that so and so was well served, they will come here."

"Don't worry," I answered, "I am sure we will be good to the community and will help a great deal of people. God willing." Inside, I worried we needed more people in our small nonprofit.

We eventually increased our staff. With Ann and Mercy gone, we needed more qualified people. I had asked one of our active and busy volunteers to work with us. Ines

Ramiro was a beautiful woman who had obtained her legal permanent status through what is known as VAWA (Violence Against Women Act of 1994).[4] She had finally divorced her husband and was saddled as a single mother to take care of her four children, all rapidly growing into their adulthood, sometimes with more problems than she bargained for. But the rock of her existence was her faith, and that solved all problems. Then there was Miriam Felix, who had gained her legal permanent residence through marriage to a U.S. citizen, Gary Fisher. And after three years, she had applied for and was granted citizenship. Miriam was an artist, a dramatic and lovely young woman who felt things deeply and told you about it. She did not hold back and was very honest, and a beautiful person. I had always said that when Miriam joined our office, it was like the sun entering the agency. She brought about lively and vibrant feelings and expressions, always compassionate with our clients, seeing that she was the first one to see them when they entered. She was our volunteer, but a girl Friday as well, because she filed all the files and knew at the tips of her fingers who was who and where their files were, an indispensable person.

"Diana." She came in one day with paper flowers and walked into my office. "I want to donate these to the office. We need more color aside from your paintings. How about if I put these throughout?" I looked up at her and laughed. "As long as we do not have to water them, that is fine. I have

---

[4] *The ACT was passed with broad bipartisan support in 1994 cosponsored by Senators Joe Biden (D-DE) and Orin Hatch (R-UT). The ACT was to see some changes and just barely be reauthorized in 2019.*

a terrible green thumb." She shook her head and wandered off into the backroom.

At times, we would joke with Tomas that he was the only man around, seeing that the fifth person to join our small office staff was our bookkeeper, Christy Edwards, a woman who had worked at the local library and had kept the books for her husband's business. Both Christy and Ines were soft-spoken and kept to themselves. Tomas was also reserved, but Miriam and I were the extroverts.

Miriam was working with us, a volunteer, so we needed a full-time secretary. I remembered one of my citizenship students and called her to see if she was interested. Funny how things happen, she was looking for a job. Soon, Karina Robles joined us and became part of our team.

Days and months had passed, and our business thrived. However, I was the only one accredited with Ann gone, and I began to feel the pinch. I could take on just so many cases and keep good management of them. I decided to spend a little money and invited Tomas to come with me to the Annual Convening of CLINIC in Washington, D.C. that May.

"Tomas." I walked over to his desk one day. "I think it's time you prepare to become an Accredited Representative."

He looked up from his desk, a bit surprised. "Of course, I would love that! I was wondering to ask you if I could start seeing clients for the Consular Process?"

I was surprised. The Consular Process would be an uncomplicated process, but there were many grounds of inadmissibility regarding when they entered and how they entered the United States, how many times, etc. It looked easy, but could be tricky. I looked at him with a bit of amazement. Here was a young man not afraid to jump into the complex path of immigration. Everyone else I had asked to join me, never really wanted to, except for Ann. She had enjoyed it very much and found it as rewarding as I did.

"Ok, I have seen you reading and looking up things, and I am sorry I have not given you my total attention, but before you do that, I want to invite you to a weeklong training. It is in Washington, D.C., all expenses paid."

His mouth opened wide in a smile, "Of course! That would be great!"

"Well, you would have to be away from your family for a whole week. Will your wife be ok with that?"

He waved his hand in the air, "Oh, no problem. She will be fine."

I was pleasantly surprised when he not only accepted but was genuinely excited about going. The trip would provide him with a week of intensive immigration training while giving me the perfect opportunity to show him around my favorite city, Washington, D.C. had always captivated me—whether it was the weight of its history, or the unmistakable presence of government power concentrated in one place, I wasn't sure. But I knew one thing for certain: I was determined to take him to the landmarks that mattered most to me—Congress, the White House, and beyond.

When we arrived, spring was in full bloom, wrapping the city in its most dazzling display of color. Everywhere we looked, flowers spilled from gardens and lined the streets. The azaleas, which had burst into bloom weeks earlier, still clung to life in some corners, their beauty lingering just a little longer. Their delicate petals, painted in soft pinks and deep magentas, tumbled gracefully into one another—like carefree children giggling as they played. It was breathtaking.

Later that day, I invited Tomas to walk with me around the Lincoln Memorial. We strolled through the space, taking in the solemn grandeur of the monument while watching crowds gather, posing for photos, and soaking in the historical significance. It was a perfect beginning to our time in the nation's capital.

"Ok, I want a photo with you, he said, and he looked around to ask a passerby to take our photo. Most people in D.C. are kind and used to tourists. One such person obliged, and we had our photo taken. Tomas was 29 years old, and I looked like his grandma in the picture. We both laughed. "Ok, time to show you my favorite places."

We walked to the metro and took the ride to Congress. I had gotten passes from our State Senator, the Honorable Dick Lugar, and we were ushered into the hallways of the upper side of the building, leading to the gallery. My dream had been to see the Congressmen and Senators in session, but the reality was that hardly anyone was in the House or in the Senate. I was not thrilled; there was no one in sight. It was disappointing, but our day of playing hooky from the Conference paid off in historical knowledge and civics as I explained to Tomas how our government worked.

"Tomas, before we go back to the hotel, I invite you to some wonderful Bolivian empanadas called Salteñas. You will love them." I led him to the site. Salteñas are savory pastries filled with beef, pork, or chicken mixed in a sweet, slightly spicy sauce containing olives, raisins, and potatoes. And as far as I knew, this place had the best. We were lucky to try them.

"Really yummy," Tomas muttered, taking a bite of the morsel. I nodded my head, too busy eating mine.

After savoring the delicious empanada-style popovers, we returned to our hotel, where the event was taking place. This was Tomas' first time to experience this type of convening, and I spent time presenting him to former colleagues.

I had caught sight of a former colleague, Sister Carmen, from the sisters of St. Benedict who lived two hours away from us and was also involved in immigration.

"Sister Carmen!" I cried out and went to hug her. She walked up to me and hugged me. "Oh, it is so good to see you!"

"Here," I pushed Tomas out in front of me, "this is our recruit, Tomas Salinas, he is working towards his Accreditation."

"Oh, that is wonderful." She turned to a young woman at her side, "And this is Sister Nancy Mueller, she is joining me in my office and is new to this as well."

"Oh, good, we are all going to learn a lot. I know how fast and furious it is, but fascinating."

"Right," countered Sister Carmen. Her eyes squinted as she smiled, "So much fun to be here together. The best part is taking it all back and helping more people."

"Amen to that," I answered enthusiastically. "I know that most talented lawyers kind of scoff at these events." I was thinking of Matt when I commented. "But for us, they are lifesavers. I remember the first time I came to one of these, I was so uninformed. And now, it is great when I understand what they are talking about!"

Sister Carmen laughed and agreed. "Yes, and they go so fast! You must really pay attention, and they are great teachers." Then, she took my arm and guided me to the side of the room. "I have something to tell you."

"Sure, what?"

"It's about Saul." His name struck a chord; of course, he had been living with them, and for months, I had been with him, interpreting for him at all his meetings with Laura, the lawyer.

"What has happened?" I was almost afraid to ask.

She smiled, her eyes shining. "He is fine. The FBI had come to question him, and we had not heard anything, and yesterday they came to tell him that they had apprehended two men thought to be part of the coyote group that had been harassing and persecuting him."

"Oh, sister," I cried excitedly. "That is great! No, that is more than great! That means he can now look for a place to live and start to live, normally?"

Sister Carmen laughed, "Yes, absolutely! And it seems he will be getting his work permit soon, and he tells me that the lawyer told him his family may be coming next year to live with him."

As we chatted, one of our teachers, lawyer Ann Smithers, walked up to us, and we gave each other a hug. "So good to see you." Ann was one of the leading instructors, a teacher, clear and concise. She was also one of the leading attorneys for CLINIC and was from the San Francisco office. We chatted for a bit after everyone was introduced and then quickly walked to our various seminars. The day had begun. I had suggested the courses Tomas should take, and then the ones for both of us to be in. We sauntered off to our workshops.

Later that night, I went to bed tired but happy to know the news about Saul, no more fear, he could live a normal life. I was also happy that Tomas had been well indoctrinated into the new field of work he would do to assist others. He was happy to be there, taking it all in and learning as much as he could. He knew it would take these events and a great deal of study before he could apply to become an Accredited Representative. But he was well on his way.

After a week of intense training and meeting people from all over the country, there were 300 affiliates in attendance. We returned to our city with the resolve that we would do our very best to assist our community and anyone who was an immigrant who needed our help. The week's one-hour sessions, the forums, and the conferences were all worthwhile. It was a short time to learn a great deal. Not only were we offered Immigration Law, but we were also offered policy information from the actual heads of government and their agencies' staff on how things ran and what the logjams or successes were. We were able to interact not only with other service providers, but also with the heads of government who dictated policy. However, when they were confronted with our questions, they did not always answer to our satisfaction.

As a former trainer, I knew that the best use of our money was to return and recycle our learning with our staff. For a week, I scheduled one-hour sessions where both Tomas and I shared with them the knowledge we had gained and insight into the various processes. Everyone was included, whether they were accredited or not. I wanted everyone to be familiarized with the work and what it involved. Plus, the pitfalls we had to avoid at all costs. This opportunity also gave Tomas the ability to share and therefore internalize what he had learned. I knew I had a star in the making.

And sure enough, it was not long before Tomas began taking on clients for consultations and working independently. He would come back and consult with me, but by and large, he began to really acquire the expertise of the law. I was happy and relieved that at last, we had a potentially good lawyer in the making.

In the meantime, the rest of the staff were carving their own niches. Ines was an adaptive learner, and she sat in the same office as Tomas, so she became his assistant. It turned out Tomas was not only a quick learner, but also a great teacher. His theory was "learn as you do." I am old-school; I like to teach first and then have them do. But whatever methodology is used, as long as our office worked efficiently, we succeeded. The two of them started cranking out the Consular Processes as hot pancakes.

One day, I called everyone in for a training session. I did not do these often due to the pressure of seeing clients and finishing cases; there was never any time.

"Ok," I began, "Today I want to cover several things with all of you. To those of you who are working on cases and at the front desk, you must give out answers if we are busy. You all need to know this." Everyone was looking intently.

I started off, "One thing is what our office does and wants to do, and another is what the immigration service does. The immigration service plays a significant role in policy development. So, if the existing administration wants to move things, things move. If they want to delay, things are delayed."

"What sort of delays?" Tomas asked.

"Well," I answered, "we understand that there are thousands, millions of petitions that must be processed carefully. But sometimes, there is a great hold up in the initial days of the process, which are the delays by the F.B.I. Once a client goes to have his fingerprints taken, the wait period to continue that case can be months. And, then, there is the problem of retrogression."

"What is retrogression?" Asked Ines.

I replied, "The number of visas issued to foreigners seeking entrance to the U.S. as legal residents (obtaining a Green Card) is set each year by the Immigration and Nationality Act (INA). But it is the Department of State (DOS) that allocates immigrant visas. In general, family-sponsored preference visas are limited to 226,000 visas per year, and employment-based visas are limited to 140,000 per year. Between these two categories, there is a subset of categories, which then diminishes the number of visas available. These are visas available to people around the world, even though there is a preference for countries other than China, India, Mexico, and the Philippines, because these countries have so many more applications than the rest of the world."

"But where does retrogression come in?" Questioned Tomas.

I replied, "When a family files a petition for a family member, that petition will arrive at the offices of immigration at a set date. Once received, it is given that date as its 'priority date.' And based on this priority date, the group of applications moves in the process through all the various steps, only by the number of available visas. According to the subset category your application is filed under, your case moves. And if the demand spikes up and there are no more visas available for that given year, it falls into a waiting list or backlog."

"So, then the dates are changed for the availability of visas, and what could be one date one day may suddenly change to a wait of years?" He asked.

I was pleased, "Exactly. You now must explain to your client that you are sorry and that their priority date is not up to date anymore and has fallen back a couple of years, and they must wait."

"Oh, my goodness," cried Miriam.

Tomas looked disgusted. "I bet that is why so many come undocumented because they are tired of waiting."

"Yes, I would venture to say that the millions that are here fall into that category. Not the ones who enter with visas, but the ones who come in undocumented."

We discussed a bit more about the ins and outs of other situations and ended the session. I was very pleased with how easily the team was incorporating the knowledge of the complex workings of immigration. We were all growing.

One day, Tomas walked into my office excited. "Diana, oh my God, we have a family held up in Juarez."

"Oh no," I was horrified. "Why? For how long?"

Tomas could barely speak, "For three years." My head was reeling. Ismael Sanchez had just turned 20 years old, and we had sought a waiver of inadmissibility. But it had been approved, and all he needed was the interview in Juarez, and that was it.

I could not believe it. "But how is it that he is stuck in Mexico for three years! Oh, my goodness, why?!"

"I really do not know. His mother called and wanted to talk to you, but you were busy."

Watching me intently, he reached forward and asked, "Diana, explain to me again, why did he have to seek a waiver of inadmissibility?"

I was also upset and wanted answers, but I would have to wait for Mrs. Sanchez to return and tell me what happened. I replied, "Because he entered without any documentation when he was 18. He obviously did not qualify for DACA. By having acquired illegal status, he had to seek permission to be allowed admissibility. Seeking a pardon."

Tomas shifted his feet, "And so even though he has paid the money, or his family paid money for his whole process, even the waiver, he is now stuck in Mexico."

"Well, something must have happened at the consular interview. And not only is he stuck, but his mother also must return, and his whole family is here, and she will have to leave him there until he seeks his re-entrance."

"So, what will she do? What will he do?"

I shook my head, "I do not know Tomas, but they are in a quandary. As far as I know, there are no family members in Mexico. He will be there alone. The problem is that now that he is 20 years old, he was barely going to make it before he aged out. Now, if he waits three years, he will age out, and that means that he will have to wait ten or twenty more years because he falls into a different category."

"Oh my God," Tomas cried out. We were both upset. Tomas was beginning to internalize our client's predicaments more and more, and I was worried he would begin stressing out.

"Look, Tomas, take this as a learning moment. We cannot internalize all our clients' problems. We do our best to avoid as many as possible, but immigration work comes with stress. Do not let it get to you." I looked aside. "I have ended up in the ER three times already due to client concerns. Do not want that to happen to you."

Tomas shook his head, "No, Diana, I will not let it get to me. I promise." With that, he stood up and walked out of the office.

I agreed. It was an awful shame, but really, there was nothing we could do. All I had to do was wait to hear from Ana Maria Sanchez, Ismael's mother, and find out what happened and what she had done.

Ana Maria was married to a U.S. citizen, Frank Farr, and she had gained her legal permanent residence through him, but he had not been able to apply for her son, as a stepson, because they had gotten married months after he had turned 18 years old. Ana Maria quickly applied for her son, but legal residents have their cases move more slowly than those of citizens; therefore, when he reached 19 years, he had to apply for the inadmissibility waiver, and it was approved two months after he was 20 years old. They had managed to jump all the hoops and hurdles, but no one had foreseen this setback.

By the skin of his teeth, he had missed his chance. In the snap of a finger, his life had changed drastically. No one to turn to, nothing to do, but wait. That evening, I went home very troubled. There was nothing I could do, but I knew all too well what would happen. That night, before I went to bed, I took out my diary:

I am so upset with the case of Ismael Sanchez. His entire family is here; he has no one in Mexico but his old grandparents. Mexico is not his home. His home is where his family is, where he has gone to school, and where he has his girlfriend. These are the many reasons why young people do not wait in their homeland to have another opportunity to return to the United States. This is one of the reasons so many come back and enter without documents. Being alone in a land of not their own choosing is too strange and too formidable. So, they make the trip back, regardless of the risks, regardless of the possibility of getting caught. They must make every effort and fight every chance to return home.

Chapter 13

ENGLISH AS A SECOND LANGUAGE

One of the key initiatives we introduced in our new office was English classes for immigrants. During our time in the Ministry, we had offered numerous classes, with Hispanic students coming and going. Some persevered and successfully passed the GED (General Education Diploma), advancing to college and expanding their opportunities. I had always believed strongly that immigrants should learn English if they intended to make this country their home. Not only would it empower them in their daily lives, but it would also ease the burden on those constantly translating letters, filling out applications, and assisting them with tasks they could handle independently if they made the effort to learn.

Despite being in the United States for ten to twenty years, many in the community had never learned English. Surrounded by Spanish speakers—whether at work or in their neighborhoods—they never felt the need or desire to invest the time. In environments where bilingual individuals are accommodated, the motivation to learn dwindles, making it easy to rely on familiarity rather than actively acquiring new skills.

However, among our students, a few stood out—particularly those of Asian descent. They arrived with an unwavering thirst for knowledge and a deep determination to improve their English. Many worked in nail salons throughout the city, speaking only fragmented English, but they persisted. Our morning classes were filled with Asian students, attending diligently for two hours before rushing off to work. They returned each session, steadily building their language skills until they could converse with confidence. Their dedication was inspiring, proving that with commitment, progress was always within reach.

One morning, I walked into our office and saw that in the classroom in the back, it was full of students, and among them a large group of negroes. I asked my staff who they were, and they answered, "From Congo."

"Really?" I was impressed and pleased, now I would have the opportunity to try out my very rusty French.

Everyone in the family had come to class. The mother, *Mamy*, was tall, thin, and beautiful. She had two older daughters, a son about seventeen, and a younger son about 12. The father and other members of the family were at work. They had no transportation, so I decided to pick them up for class, which was on my way to the office, and then at noon, I took them home. It was not a big deal; these were refugees, and we could at least help in that way. Besides, it gave me the opportunity to practice my French. Mamy was kind, and she frequently smiled when she corrected me. I did notice that the older kids were not as forgiving. I was butchering the language, and they winced, but she smiled. We did this for months, but I have to say, with her corrections and my insistence on bettering my French, I did improve. I tried not to be curious about them, but I must admit, I was curious as to why they were here in Indiana, of all places, and why they had to leave Congo. But I never asked, and they never told me. I soon learned that refugees do not like to talk about their travails. And quite frankly, I had so much on my mind that it did not matter. As long as they were learning the language and this was improving their lives, that was all that mattered.

During this, one morning, Ana Maria Sanchez walked into my office. After what had happened, I had expected her to visit me following the event, but it was months before she did.

"Ana Maria, how are you? How is Ismael?" She looked shyly at me. "Señora Diana, he is back."

"What?"

"Yes, he remained in Mexico a couple of months and decided he could not stay any longer, and he found his way back. His whole experience was somewhat traumatic. He tried to work a bit, and he earned enough to get himself across back through Arizona."

"Did you know he was coming back?" I looked at her intently.

She smiled. "Yes, I figured he would. He has a girlfriend, and I knew that he would not stay down there, and she is here. Both are young and in love."

"Right." I could only imagine. I could not help but think, *one more for the statistics.*

"So now that he has returned, what is he going to do?"

"Well..." She hesitated. Then, forging ahead, replied, "That is why I am here. I want your advice on what he should do."

I let out a laugh. "Advice! Ana Maria, legally, he should not be here. He is now in deep trouble."

I tried to explain, "Having gone out of the country is as if he self-deported. So now the government wants him to return to Mexico and wait until he can return legally, even if it takes 20 to 30 years. He has broken the law coming back, and now if they stop him, they will deport him, and he will not be allowed back in permanently. That's immigration law."

She slapped her hand on her knee, "But that is crazy!"

I shook my head and said, "Yes, I know. There are many things that should be changed in immigration law, and this is one of them, but so far, until it does, there is no recourse. But tell me what happened. Why did they deny his visa?"

She took a deep breath. "When he went to his medical exam, they asked him if he had ever smoked Marijuana. And he said he had tried it once just to see what it was like. And with that admonition, they denied his petition. Once in the interview, they told him he was denied for three years."

I looked at her and shook my head, "So, for telling the truth and acknowledging having tried it once, it was sufficient for them to deny his petition?"

Ana Maria replied quietly, "Yes, they did."

We always advise our clients to tell the truth. I just wish he had told us about this, but it had never been important since he had only tried it like so many other thousands of teenagers do.

I stood up, went around my desk, and gave Ana Maria a hug. "I am so sorry this has happened. He is paying the consequences of his youthful mistake. I am afraid there is not much we can do right now. I am sorry."

She walked to the door and said, "Ok then. Thank you. I will tell him to take care."

"That is good, Ana Maria. I am really so sorry for all of this."

With that, she turned and walked out. I stared at the figure as she walked out, saddened by the twists and turns of the law and the gyrations people had to do to somehow try to straighten out their lives and continue in normalcy.

Our office sailed through the months ahead with a great deal of work, and after our English classes, we began computer learning, and on Saturdays, with U.S. History and Civics classes, we were busy.

Then one sunny day, three beautiful Black women were waiting for me when I entered my office. They were my 10 am appointment, and I was late. I apologized, and after getting settled in my office, I called them in.

They were also from the Congo, friends of Mamy's family, and wanted to learn how to become U.S. citizens. The mother was very quiet and almost shy, though from her two daughters, I gathered that she was a force to be reckoned with. They shared some of their story with me.

Karisha spoke, "Our entire family came to the U.S. as refugees, and we had to wait for two years to be given the go-ahead and obtain the visa to come here, and then our residency."

Like most immigration processes, becoming a refugee is not easy and takes a process of vetting before they are considered for the visa.

"Once in the United States," she continued, "Both our mom, Victoria, and our dad, Willy, decided to separate." She looked down. "The marriage was not going well, and we left with her to come to Indiana, and our brother, Idowu stayed with our father."

I would later find out that this was going to be problematic because Willy did not offer Victoria any information as to where they moved to and what their phone number was, and made it difficult for her to reach her son and talk to him.

I looked at Karisha. "And where is your older sister? There is just you and Monica."

"On our way to board the plane for America." She shifted nervously in her seat. "Our older sister was not allowed to board by her husband, and she had to remain behind, leaving all of us grief-stricken." She reached to pat her mother's hand, "Especially our mom."

Whatever they were running away from, she now had to worry about her older daughter remaining in a country with civil unrest and a husband who would lord his might over his wife. It reminded me of the Macho Latino. I just shook my head.

"Ok, Victoria." I smiled at them and continued, "I am willing to teach you U.S. History and Civics every Wednesday from 4 pm to 5 pm. Is that a good time?"

They all nodded in agreement. "I work at Amazon and may come in late," said Monica. "Well then, give me another time."

"Could we do it in the morning, like now?"

I had no problem with that, so we established they would come every Wednesday for their History class. They already knew English, so it would be easy. They came from Kinshasa, in the Democratic Republic of Congo, one of the main cities where a great deal of strife had taken place. Their area had seen a turnover from Belgian leaders to African leaders, with corruption a constant throughout their history as a colony of Belgium, and later violence toward women, rape being a weapon of war.[5] I was not going to imagine what, if anything, they had gone through. I knew little of the history of the Congolese Republic, but I did remember reading about the Rwandan genocide between the Tutsis and Hutus. Just imagining that they may have had to run from such genocide made me shudder. And I was not going to ask them.

Every Wednesday morning, as scheduled, the three women appeared, ready to study. I had them sit in the large

---

5   *Rape as a Weapon of War in Congo*, originally published in *Spiegel International*.

classroom and would sometimes have to make a point and write something on the blackboard.

Monica was the playful one and sometimes had interesting questions. Karisha was quieter, but more astute and intelligent. She seldom spoke, but when she did, she was direct and to the point. Their mother, Victoria, was a lovely, kind person. She was almost shy in her answers, but I felt a strong bond among them. After 14 weeks, I had gone from the early Pioneer days through Revolution, the Civil War, the Industrial Age, and modern history. All in all, pointing out that our country had been founded on the premise that we were all created equal, a promise, however, I felt we had yet to deliver. With fits and starts, we had tried and in 244 years still had not obtained our goal. Somehow, moving close to that perfect union had eluded us up to now. They listened quietly, never ever saying how bad things had been in their country. I usually had my students participate and give opinions; none of the three women ever did. Even Monica, who was the most extroverted, never said much in terms of their country, their situation, or what they were experiencing in the States. With my students, I had interesting discussions, but with these women, there were none.

Unfortunately, with them, I could not incorporate their history into the timeline covered in U.S. History because I knew nothing about the Congo's history. But we sailed through those months, them asking some questions and my telling them what had happened when and why. When we finished the history and civics part, I had to review with them what the interview would be like. This was when things began to be said, and I began to understand a little about them.

"Victoria, the officer is going to ask you why your oldest daughter did not come with you if you were seeking asylum and obviously running away from a bad situation, maybe even a dangerous situation. What are you going to tell him or her?"

Victoria looked at me and looked down. Then she said softly, "Because her husband would not let her come with us."

"But you were in danger, and so was she. Why would he stop her from fleeing to a safe place?"

Before Victoria spoke, Monica chimed in, "Because in Congo, men rule, and we do as they say."

"What?" I asked incredulously. "Men do and say, and women have to obey blindly?"

All three of them answered in unison, "Yes."

"Hmm." I looked at them and said, "I do not know how the officers will take that. Perhaps you will have to educate them, Victoria, and explain to them about how your society deals with women and the relationship between men and women. I assume it is very strong."

They all nodded their heads.

"How did it happen? Did you wait for her, and she did not show up?"

"Yes, we waited weeks, and our plane was departing, and we had to go or stay, so we left. My husband said we needed to go." Victoria's eyes began to fill with tears, and I began to feel very uncomfortable. Perhaps things are best not said. I reached out with a box of Kleenex and continued the prepping.

"Ok, we will end there for today. But we must practice your answers. Ok?" They all nodded.

Days passed, and we kept practicing until finally, the citizenship interview for all came. I had waited for Karisha, Monica, and Victoria at my office, and when they arrived, we went in my car, and I drove them to Indianapolis for the citizenship interview. I was going as the Accredited Representative, to sit and listen and not say a word unless something was out of line, or I needed to ask questions. Technically, I was going to advocate for her if needed to. But I knew that advocating was a sensitive and careful situation. I would have to intervene only if things got out of hand, and I had to defend my client.

Once we entered the building, we took the elevator to the tenth floor and went through security. After passing through, I guided them to the windows where they submitted their interview letters. The officer looked at them and waved them out into the seating area and said, "You will be called, go sit down."

We sat down and waited, no one saying anything. The first one called out was Victoria. I stood up and walked in with her, told the officer who I was, and we were ushered into his office. The man looked Latino, with burly black hair, a white complexion, and a stocky body. His last name was Sanchez, but he did not say much until we entered the office, and he closed the door. He asked us to remain standing. Then he asked Victoria to raise her right hand and swear to tell the truth and nothing but the truth; she did, and he motioned her to sit down. He looked at me and asked me for my identification, so I had my driver's license ready, and I handed it to him. He took it and motioned me to sit down. He then looked at his two monitors, entered something in his computer, and turned to Victoria and asked her for her passport, her Green Card, and her driver's license.

"I have no driver's license, I do not drive," Victoria replied.

He was still staring at his computer, "How did you get here, then?"

I interjected, "I drove the family here, Officer."

"That is fine, but let the petitioner answer, please." He looked directly at me. I felt like someone had slapped my hand.

He turned to her. "I am going to ask you some questions about your application, and then I will ask you some questions about history and civics. If you answer six correctly, you will have passed the test. Do you understand?"

Victoria nodded her head. He said, "Good, let's start with the history and civics." He began to ask her questions from his computer site, and she answered all correctly. He wrote some more into his computer, and then he leaned back on his chair with her file opened in front of him.

"Ok, that was good. You have answered all six questions correctly. I am going to ask you some questions about your application. I have a red pen to change whatever was written in error and make those changes. You are to answer truthfully and correctly."

His whole attitude was intimidating. She had already sworn she would answer truthfully, but he acted like a bully. I was beginning to not like him, but had to keep my cool.

He started asking the usual normal questions; her name, address, and so forth, and everything was going smoothly until he came across her naming all her children. When she came to the eldest's address, she told him she had not come with them. This appeared to bother the officer, and he looked at her sternly, "And why did she not come with you? Your visa is one for refugees. She saw you were fleeing your country, and she suddenly did not want to come with you. She was safe, and you were not?" I felt tension.

Victoria looked sad and softly said, "In Congo, it is not the women's right to say what they want. My daughter is married, and her husband did not want her to come with us."

"But did he not know that you were waiting to get your visa, maybe for some years, before you could come?"

"Yes, he said it was fine for us, but not his wife. She had to remain with him."

"Even if her life was in danger?"

Victoria began to get emotional. She whispered, "Yes."

The officer remained silent and looked at the file. "What about your son's address. You wrote down that you do not know. Don't you love your son? Do you not talk to him?"

Victoria looked at me, and I wanted to take her hand and calm her down but could not. I felt like intervening would not be right, but I had already been barked at and did not want to make my client's position more difficult. I whispered, "Tell him."

She straightened up and looked straight at him. "When my husband and I came to this country we were carrying many marital problems. After a few months, we realized we could no longer live together, so we decided to separate. He was to take our son, Idowu, and the two girls. So, I moved to Indiana, and he moved and did not tell me where to or how to reach him."

"So basically, your husband has vanished into thin air."

"No," she replied softly, "My daughter, Monica, talks to him."

He closed her file and leaned forward. "Ms. Victoria, I am going to give you a chance to succeed with your application. I want you to find your husband and find out your son's address. Then you can come back and try again. For now, we are finished."

With that, he stood up, and we stood up, and I followed him out of the office, out in the lobby, where her daughters were waiting and looking worried when they saw her. I told them to not say anything, and I walked quickly out of the area and out to the elevators. Once we were in the elevators, everyone began talking, and I calmed them down.

"No, she did not fail; she will have to return to answer some questions about your brother." I turned to Monica, "You will have to call your father and find out his address and your brother's phone number, and we will be good."

Victoria was crying, and the girls were hugging her. It had been painful, and the officer did not have to be that harsh with her. I was mad and trying to keep my emotions in control because the other three women were all talking fast and furious in French, and I was upset too.

When we returned to the office, I made them promise they would call me with the information on the husband and the son. They walked off to their car, still talking excitedly in French. I did not understand, nor was I trying to, and walked into my office and said goodbye to them. As I walked in, our receptionist, Karina, excitedly told me there was a gentleman who did not have an appointment but had to see me. I turned around and saw a tall Black man with what looked like intense pain on his face. I asked him to give me a few minutes, and I would call him in; with this, I walked ahead to my office and straightened some things before I called him in.

His skin was so dark, it was blue, beautifully blue. His eyes were wide in pain, and his mouth was red, his lips opening to show a straight row of white teeth. I was taken aback by his stature and his elegance. He may have been dressed raggedly, but he carried himself well. I smiled at him and motioned for him to sit down in the chair in front of my desk.

"Please, what can I do for you?" I began. He closed his eyes for a minute and said in a whimper, "I don't know if you can do anything for me, but you are my last hope."

"Well," I replied, "I will do whatever I can."

"I will tell you from the beginning."

"Please do," I replied.

"I am an immigrant. I come from Namibia, Africa. I came as a refugee and now, I am a United States citizen."

"Wonderful," I replied, truly glad that he had achieved this all-important goal that all immigrants aspire to reach.

"I have been working for Krammer's. I pick up boxes from the delivery vans and must run to place them on pallets. I work 10 hours a day, seven days a week."

"What?" I said in dismay. "This is not legal. You must have breaks."

He smiled jeeringly, "No ma'am, that does not exist. You do what they say, or you are fired. We become their slaves."

All I could think of was how this could not be. There are laws governing how many hours people work, have breaks, and have time to eat. This is part of our labor laws. How could this be?

"Well," he continued. "I slipped and fell last year and broke my back. I was taken to a clinic, and then I was assigned to see a chiropractor. But the chiropractor said I needed to see a back surgeon because I had serious spine injuries."

"These were the medical facilities that cover Workman's Comp?"

"I guess, so, I only went wherever they told me to go. I was in a lot of pain. I had to have something done. I have three children and a wife and must support them."

"What happened after you saw an orthopedic surgeon?"

"He said I needed three surgeries."

"And did you undergo these surgeries?"

"Yes, but each time it was a fight, because my social worker said that the company could not keep on paying for all of these surgeries."

I waved my hand aside, dismissing this. "Yes, but that is the law. Workman's Comp must cover the injured worker and have that worker see all the doctors it needs until he is finally evaluated, found he is fine, and can return to work.'

"Oh, they told me I was fine and could go back to work after the first surgery. But I could not. I could not move, and I could not do any more lifting." Every time he protested, his eyes widened and his mouth opened wide. He was a picture of indignation and pain.

"Ma'am, I am a human being, and they treat me like garbage because I am an immigrant, and I am Black." I winced at his words.

These cases always made me angry. The abuse of the companies and the insurance companies that assist the injured worker always works in tandem. Seldom does it really benefit the injured worker. I had experienced many that had this happen. Eventually, they settle just to be done with the battle and try to go off on their own and get healed elsewhere. But they paid the brunt of it, in money and in pain and health.

"Well, Mr. Condy, you may have to sue the company and the insurance company."

"Oh, that is a waste of time. I have gone to all the best lawyers in two cities, and no one will take my case. They say they cannot do anything. Or are too busy and do not have time. No one." Then he looked at me intently. "That is why I am here. You are my final hope. Your organization works with immigrants, and maybe you can help me. I have had two surgeries, but they refuse to do the third. The third is close to my neck, and I suffer greatly."

My heart and head said, "Yes," but frankly, I did not know how. I turned to my phone and called a colleague with whom we collaborated. I got his secretary, "Hi Genny, this is Diana. Who does Matt use for Workman's Comp cases?" I quickly took down the name and number, thanked her, and hung up. Then I dialed the number. It was the State's Refugee Human Rights Council. No one answered, it was a machine with many to-go-to's and I hung up.

"Look, I am going to have to call again until I talk to somebody. This group fights for the human rights of immigrants, so perhaps they can help us, and if not, refer us to someone who can."

He looked at it, relieved, and for the first time, he smiled. As he smiled, his eyes glowed. I knew I had to help this man.

I reached out my hand to him and grabbed his. "Look, I am going to find someone who can help you. You need to fight this and seek this surgery and some form of compensation. Back injuries are serious, and how this will affect your working life, I do not know, but as you said, you have a family to feed and shelter."

He reached out to grab my hand and strongly squeezed, "Yes, Ma'am. Thank you, Ma'am. You will call me?

"Yes, I will. Today is Friday, I will try Monday morning and call your home."

"I will be there." He stood up and slowly walked out of my office.

As he walked out, I muttered under my breath, "Damn." This wasn't the first time. I had seen it before—workers crushed by collapsing walls due to negligence, employers eager to shift responsibility. I recalled a woman who was injured in a recycling plant, slipping on unattended slime, twisting her foot so badly she could no longer walk. I had accompanied her to therapy appointments, observing the cold indifference of medical professionals who seemed more focused on minimizing her complaints than addressing her pain.

Time and time again, I witnessed the same dismissive attitude. It was as if these workers—immigrants who had labored tirelessly—were merely exaggerating, lying, or whining. But I knew better. I had seen their injuries, understood their struggles, and felt the quiet rage that built inside me as they were belittled. It was all about money, about avoiding accountability, about the unspoken resistance to truly caring for immigrant patients. The discomfort was visible—in the eyes of nurses, the clipped tones of receptionists, the distant formality of doctors. Legally, they did the bare minimum, signed the forms, declared patients "fine," while those patients, in turn, told me they were anything but fine. They weren't seeking payouts or exploiting the system. They just wanted to heal, to return to their normal lives—or as close to normal as they could get.

I often wondered—*had anyone studied how many immigrant workers have been injured on the job without being properly treated, fully healed, or fairly compensated?* I doubted it. Who would care enough to investigate? In our Midwestern state, the prevailing sentiment was clear: immigrants were tolerated, but never truly valued. The only places I had seen genuine concern were within the schools, where teachers cared deeply. Outside of that, the community seemed to merely accept their presence because they needed them, for the labor others refused to do. Unlike the small towns in Ohio and elsewhere that rallied around their immigrant neighbors, here in Indiana, people kept their distance, unwilling to engage.

I thought back to a conversation with my neighbor. She had given me a knowing look and said, "You must not like our president too much." I just shook my head. There was no point in arguing. Minds were made up. Hearts were closed. When did we stop acknowledging that we are all descendants of immigrants? When did we start believing that we were purely American, as though we hadn't all come from somewhere else? I shook my head again, lost in the weight of that thought.

That was the last I saw of Mr. Condy. I tried calling the Refugee office and never got to talk to a human. It was always the machine. Machines made me irritable. I could not complain to them or ask them anything. His visit left me with many misgivings. I knew we were limited in what we could do for our clients, but somehow injustice like this really troubled me.

A few weeks after Victoria's interview, we received another appointment letter. I called her and told her I would take her again to ensure that she was not coerced or had the same interviewer. She agreed, and on the appointed day, she and Monica showed up in my office.

On our way to the immigration office, we chatted, and she had the number and address of her son and was very happy because she had called him and talked to him. I could tell that having done that gave Victoria a great deal of pride; she had overcome her fear and had talked to her husband. The male dominance in any society was a very sore spot in my life. Any human dominance over another was a sore spot in my life. I could not stand it, and it made me very mad. Whether they were Latino machos or Congolese machos did not sit well with me. But for now, we had what we needed, and hopefully she would have a different interviewer.

It was not long after we checked in that the interviewer came to the door and called out her name. I sighed in relief; it was another man. He was a young man, pleasant but not chatty. In all my years of dealing with immigration officers, I ran into only two who were chatty and outwardly friendly. The rest, regardless of gender, age, or ethnicity, were coolly professional and very direct. They smiled and were usually not intimidating, but were not outwardly friendly. The officer this morning was young, blonde, and he smiled widely.

"So, you were here about two months ago?" He asked, going through her file.

Victoria squirmed in her seat and softly replied, "Yes."

He was reading some notes and looked up at her, "And do you have your son's address and phone number now?"

Victoria produced a piece of paper and handed it to him, and said, "He is at 4250 Smithson Avenue in New York City. And his phone number is 212-564-8913."

He smiled. "Good. Did you talk to him?"

She smiled. "Yes, he was good. I was happy to hear him."

"I am sure you were," he replied as he looked further in her file. He closed the file, looked at her directly, and said, "Ms. Victoria, there seems to be nothing else today. I am going to recommend that you have your application for Naturalization approved."

I stood up and stretched my hand. "Thank you, Officer."

"No problem, none at all." He stood up and ushered us out of his office and out into the waiting room. "Have a good day."

With that, I walked ahead of Victoria and let her and Monica chatter excitedly as we walked out of the immigration offices.

Once in the car, Monica said, "That was all? For that, we had to take a two-hour drive and were full of nerves." I shrugged, "Yes, that's immigration."

I couldn't say more—I understood that the Service aimed to be fair and uphold the law. But now and then, there were individuals who were difficult, even outright cruel. Some of them were real jerks. The one assigned to Victoria was one of the worst. He never cut her any slack, treating her with cold suspicion, as if her entire refugee status were a sham. It was infuriating. Knowing how grueling the vetting process was, how much resilience and patience it required, made it all the more frustrating to see people forced into these circumstances—questioned, doubted, and treated as if they didn't deserve the safety they had worked so hard to obtain.

Then I turned to her, "Monica looks at the bright side. Your mom passed and will soon be a citizen. That is what you all wanted. I am proud of all of you."

Monica smiled and said, "Thank you, Ms. Diana, for your help."

"My pleasure."

With that, we remained quiet and occasionally chit-chatted back to the office. Once they left, I walked into the lobby.

"How did it go?" Asked Tomas.

"It went well, it was quick. There really was not much to say or do. I really do not know why the other guy did not ok her interview and let her pass. But then, she did it!"

Tomas laughed, "Yeah, you never know with immigration. But I am glad everything went well. Listen, if you have a minute, I want to share some information and get your opinion."

I walked into my office and motioned him to sit down." Sure, what do you have?"

"Diana, have you ever heard of a guy called Anthony?"

I frowned, "God, yes, he is a total creep. What has he done now?"

Tomas looked at me and leaned over, "How do you know him?"

"Oh, he goes back a couple of years. I had heard complaints from families that he was exploiting teenage girls, and I even tried to talk to the prosecutor about him and made a complaint. He was arrested, went to jail, and the next day he was out."

"What was the complaint about?"

"That he had young teens, boys and girls in his store, or his salon, and he exploited them for sex and other stuff."

Tomas leaned back on his chair and took a deep breath. "Well, we have another problem. He is running a sex trafficking scheme. I got this information from a client who told me all they do is make a phone call and ask if they can have an 'oil change.' And if they can, they know that it is the signal they can go ahead and pick up a teen and have sex with them, child."

"Oh my God!" I felt my stomach tighten and my heart sink. "How revolting! But it was that "oil change" thing I went to talk to the prosecutor about, and they did not seem to be interested. So that scheme is still going on?"

"Not only is it going on, but the mother of one teen called me and wants us to help her. The kid was first putting her off and said he was old enough to know what he was going through, and then called her and asked for help."

"All I can do is go by the procurator's office and try to talk to Mr. Hal personally and see what he tells me. Because Tomas, this guy is slippery, and somehow, he gets off with the law. I do not know what he has on them, or what pull he has with authorities, but this Anthony guy is a real gem. Somehow, he gets off scoot free."

Tomas stood up, "Oh, and Juanita's appointment has arrived. We must prep her."

I was swept with joy! Finally, after all these years, Juanita was going to go to Juarez and get her Green Card and come back safely. Oh, that was a win!

"That is great, Tomas. Ok, call her and get her set. I will make an appointment with the prosecutor and talk to him."

"Good." He walked out of the room smiling.

That night, I got home tired but feeling somewhat content. Happy even, because we had foiled immigration again and won, and now we had Juanita's case coming up successfully after all the coyness with her husband, who was more an ex-husband, but good enough to help us get her papers for her.

That night I wrote in my diary:

There are days when you win some and lose some. Today was a win-win. Glad about Victoria and Juanita, but worried about the teens that are in Anthony's grasp. He is an evil Panamanian who has been here for years and years and has prayed for the young. Some can run away and leave the area, like Jorge and Fiorella. Others, I never know how they ended up. I feel I have done my duty in reporting him to the police, but to no avail. I do not understand how some of these perverts get away with things. Why does the law not take them in, jail them, and throw the key away? I remember how a couple came to cry to me and told me they knew he was giving his daughter tea that drugged her and made her do things she would not have done, and then, when she ran away, he suffered from headaches and hallucinations, months after having taken the tea. I remember looking up the name of the tea and reading about its repercussions, its side effects, mostly psychological. Based on that, I had talked to Mr. Hal, the prosecutor, and he had looked at me as if I were taking something myself!! I know he did not believe me, and I had nothing to prove it. I worry that again I have nothing to prove. Maybe if the mother who called

Tomas goes with me, it would change this man's mind. Well, all I can do is try.

Chapter 14

THE CENTRAL AMERICANS

During the 2016 presidential campaign, we heard a great deal about the "Caravan" of people migrating from Central America to come and rape and violate our country. The political candidate made sure to instill fear in people, and his main agenda was to get rid of immigrants in this country; he succeeded enough to get himself elected.

After the newly elected President of the United States took office, his administration swiftly launched efforts to expel as many immigrants as possible. We were shaken when, just months into the new term, a harsh directive was announced—the "Zero Tolerance Policy." Under this new rule, no one would be allowed entry into the country without proper documentation. News of the policy spread quickly, and when reports emerged of children and families being brutally separated at the border, I was overwhelmed with emotion and a desperate urge to help. The thought of families being torn apart haunted me—I couldn't bear it. I immediately reached out to our Field Coordinator at CLINIC, asking what actions were being taken, how we might locate and reconnect families, and what other affiliates were doing in response. Her reply came swiftly: she urged me to stay put. The families, she explained, were being placed in federal prisons—making it impossible to trace them through the usual channels like DHS. However, she reassured me that, in time, some of these individuals would likely reach our state and seek support.

She was right. Before long, a family from Honduras arrived at my office. Thankfully, they had not been separated. The family consisted of two spouses and their three children, and their story was harrowing. I invited the father inside and asked if he could bring a few chairs from the classroom in the back. Once they were seated around my desk, the room felt full, filled not just with people, but with the weight of their journey. The father, Josue, remained standing. He had a calm, composed demeanor—gentle in spirit yet unmistakably resolute. His dark eyes locked with mine, framed by bushy brown hair and soft curls that tumbled forward as he leaned in slightly. In a voice that was quiet but steady, he looked at me and said, "No, not what can you do for me. What can you do for *us*?" As he spoke, he gestured softly to include his family, his words carrying the hope—and heartbreak—of them all.

I said, "Well, first let me hear your story. I need to know whether you are eligible for asylum or not. I am going to ask you a lot of questions, and then I will decide whether I can help you or not."

He sat down, smiled, and said, "OK."

I reached for my computer and began asking questions. I looked at him and spoke.

"When did you come to the United States?"

He laughed and slapped his thigh. "Oh my goodness, I came in 2005."

'WHAT," I exclaimed. "You're not eligible. You must file for asylum within the year of your entry; you are out of the possibility only if there are other circumstances that would make you eligible."

He shook his head. "No, I'm not worried about me, I'm worried about my family, my wife, my two sons, my daughter, who just came in two months ago, and they have had a very harrowing experience."

I turned to the wife and asked, "What is your name?"

Not looking at me, shyly, in a soft voice, she answered, "Maria Andrea."

Maria was a shy, quiet lady with jet black hair, a large braid to her shoulders, a fine face with fine features, a straight nose, large eyes, large eyebrows, and eyelashes. She was quite pretty, I would say, in the range of 30 to 40 years old, and in a very demure way, she began to tell me her story. She folded her hands on her lap and began speaking.

"My husband was working our fields in Honduras. We did not have much, but he made the land give fruit, and we ate and sold some of the produce that he planted."

"What did he plant?

"Oh, mostly beans, and some corn."

"And did the children help him or did they go to school?"

She sat straight, proudly, "No, they went to school. We wanted them to get ahead in life to do something different than what we did."

I smiled, "That is very good. Did you work out in the fields too?"

"Oh yes, but only for a couple of months. I harvest coffee beans, and that work is good for only three months."

"Is that in your fields?"

"Oh no, it is for a large landowner. He hires the same people every season. We go plant the beans and then spend time harvesting only three months, while the rest of the coffee beans grow. It is a slow process."

The entire time that we were talking, the family had sat intently listening to our banter. The husband smiled and seemed to motivate his wife to speak. She was lively once allowed to speak, and she went on eagerly to tell her story.

"My husband, we have lived together for close to 20 years now...."

I cut her off with, "Are you not legally married?"

She smiled, and he fidgeted. "No," she replied. I turned and looked at him as if asking for an explanation. He turned a bit red in the face and looked at me abashed. "We never had time for a wedding or the money." I did not answer. Getting married among people from rural areas in Latin America is never really about money. It is simply something that traditionally is done: two people meet, they fall in love, and decide to live together, and that is it. No need for any civil document or formality. I remember when I was young and trying to get married by the church, my fiancée and I chased after our priest to find him marrying off one hundred couples, in a big ceremony for all those who, after living together, wanted to marry. So, I was familiar with the custom. I did not like it much, but so be it.

Maria continued, "My husband has been a successful farmer, worked hard, and made a little money. Back in 2005, there were people in our neighborhood who were jealous, and they started to make trouble for him."

"What kind of trouble?" I asked.

"They were troublemakers who were starting to get involved with criminals. So, they asked him to join them and help them sell drugs or carry drugs for the big guys."

"Big guys?" I imagined large syndicates, drug lords.

She moved her head affirmatively, "Yes, the big boss was a drug lord."

"He told them to leave him alone; he was not interested."

"And did they?"

She shook her head, "No, they did not, and continued to harass him. They continued, and after having to fight them off one day, he physically fought them and escaped, running to the house."

"I told her to warn me if she saw them hanging or coming towards the house next time," Josue interjected.

"And the next day I did see them coming, so I ran out to the road and ran up to Josue and told him not to come home to go away because they were heading our way."

"When she ran to me, I decided to run to my brother's house and hide there until I decided what to do." Josue was intent in his gaze as he explained.

"How long did you stay at your brother's?" I asked.

"Oh, not long," he said. "We discussed what to do, and Jorge told me he could stave them off and talk sense to them, because we knew them; they had been neighbors for years."

"And then, you decided to come to the United States?"

"Yes," he answered.

"When my husband left, we knew because Jorge came to tell us, we had to be careful and watchful because we did not know if they would try to do something to us."

"And did they do something to you after he left?"

She answered sullenly, "Not at first. My husband started to send us money, and we continued living well. Time passed, and then one day a group of men decided to go after our oldest son, Jonatan."

"How so?" I asked, as I continued writing in my intake questionnaire.

"As our town grew and years passed, the violence in our town escalated, and soon we had young criminal gangs related to the drug traffic in our country come in and ask for 'protection or tax' money."

"What's that?" I interrupted.

"It is a way for these thugs to get money from us. If you do not pay them, they kill you."

"Oh, my goodness," I remarked.

"They began to pick on us when they stopped and hustled Jonatan after he was coming out of school."

"When was this?" I interrupted again.

"Two years ago."

"Almost fifteen years after your husband had left you?"

She nodded. "Yes, they began to push him around, and then one of them, on a motorbike, ran the bike against him and gashed his leg."

"Oh, my goodness," I cried out.

"We were warned by neighbors and rushed to aid him and found his friends had taken him to a clinic. The others had run away."

"Do you think these kids were related to the men who had previously harassed your husband?"

"Oh, I am sure," she replied firmly. "I was so scared. I am still sure that they were related. After Jonatan healed and returned to school, he continued to be followed, and finally, he came in one day and told me he was leaving. He wanted to go meet his father in the United States. He did not want to stay there any longer because he knew how things got from bad to worse."

"What did you do? Did you try to stop him?"

She looked at me, surprised. "No, how could I stop him? I knew how scared my husband had been, and now I could see the same thing with my son. No, I gave him money, blessed him, and told him to be careful. He was 17 years old, and I knew that God would take care of him for me. I hated to see him go, but felt he would be safer."

I was surprised by her resolve and faith. She had uncrossed her legs and moved forward, intent on telling her story. The others sat quietly. Jonatan rolled up his pants and let me see the large gash that had scarred his leg. His father then took some photographs from a packet of papers and showed them to me. I could see a great deal of blood over a leg. He had obviously been seriously hurt.

I turned to him, "So Jonatan, with your leg like that. How long did it take to heal so you could walk normally?"

"Oh, it took months." His green eyes glistened. He was about five feet four inches tall, heavy-shouldered, and stocky. His face was round, his smile sincere and warm. I was struck by the calmness of the entire family, the soft, softened manner of all, and their friendly and warm demeanor.

"What happened on your trip to the States?"

He shook his shoulders. "Oh, nothing much. I just followed other kids who were in Mexico and climbed the beast."[6]

My mouth opened, "Oh my God, you climbed the beast? Was that not dangerous? So many have died that way!" It was an accusation. How could he have climbed the train as it ran at great speeds down the railroad tracks? I had heard how many young kids, and some adults, tried it and managed to stay on for miles until they reached Mexico City. Along the way, there were townspeople who were ready with bags of food and knew when the train appeared, and they ran alongside, throwing bags of food for their long trip. Sometimes that was all they ate as the train sped on. I

---

[6] El tren de la muerte ("The Death Train") *refers to a network of Mexican freight trains that are utilized by U.S.-bound migrants to more quickly traverse the length of Mexico, also known as La Bestia ("The Beast") and El tren de los desconocidos ("The train of the unknowns"). It is estimated that yearly between 400,000 and 500,000 migrants, the majority of whom are from El Salvador, Guatemala, and Honduras, ride atop these trains in the effort to reach the United States.*

also had a client, a woman from Honduras, who missed her climb and had a leg run over by the train. She was picked up and taken to a hospital and remained there in that town for a year until she managed to continue her trip to the U.S. border. So, I knew how dangerous it was. Also, at one of CLINIC's convenings, I had met some Mexican nuns who aided those who had arrived on this train and saw them to a safe haven at their convents and took care of them until they could continue their trip.

Shyly, Jonatan replied, "Yes, it was dangerous, but I had no other way to make it to the U.S. border, and the money my mother had given me was quickly disappearing. I had to reach the border to call my father and get his help."

I looked at the documents he had given me. "It says here that you were detained at the entrance to the U.S. You had not sneaked in; you gave yourself up at the Port of Entry as you came to the gates."

He nodded, "Yes, and then they took me to a very cold room. It was freezing. I was there for some days and finally moved to a boy's home."

"A boy's home?" I looked at the papers and found the shelter, CASA PADRE.

"Yes, it was run by some Catholic nuns and priests. We were well treated. Then, finally, the social worker who was helping me told me they had contacted my dad, and I was taking a bus and seeing him soon."

I turned to Maria, "Well, we know now how Jonatan got here a year ago. Now, tell me what happened when you were left with the rest of your children."

Maria had leaned back in her chair, giving her son the chance to speak. She had waited quietly without correcting him or changing his story. Neither did Josue say anything. And the other two children, young teenagers, had also sat listening attentively.

"I stayed behind with what was left of my family, my children, Geovany and Lisa, who are here. Geovany is 15 years old, and Lisa is 14. My son, Geovany, came one day from school with a bag of food in his hands and invited me to eat. He told me some neighbors had given it to him. It looked good and tasted ok. I did not question him, and soon, I was frothing at the mouth, and so was he, and we were terribly sick."

"Oh, my goodness, was it poison?"

"Yes, my daughter ran to my sister's house, who did not live far from me, and she came running and quickly made a drink with lemon and coffee and made us drink. With that, she cut the poison, and then we were very sick for two days. She called my husband, and he sent money, and with the help of her husband, they took us to the hospital, which was about an hour away. There at the Hospital of San Marcos in Ocotepeque, we were finally treated and released."

"Did you file a complaint?"

"No, when we were released, I did not ask for hospital papers saying what had happened to us, and I did not file a complaint with the police because we are as afraid of the police as we are of the criminals."

"How so?" I had heard of this but wanted another opinion.

"Oh, they are sometimes as bad as the criminals and work with them. You do not want to let them know you are complaining publicly because they will tell the gangs, and then the gangs will come and kill you or torture you."

"No one in your country, no one with authority can help or will help people like you?"

"Some do, but you do not know who will; we prefer not to do it in order not to get into further trouble."

I continued writing on the computer, taking in all the information. They remained quiet as I wrote down what she had said. Once I finished, I turned to her, "Anything else happened?"

She smiled sadly, "Oh, yes. Months later, again in school, my son Geovany was assaulted by the same thugs, they are young hoodlums who had hurt Jonatan. They held him and tried to strangle him, but some of Geovany's friends heard the scuffle and ran to his aid, and they fought off the thugs. Geovany and his friends all ran to their homes. Another month passed, with my son afraid of going to school, sometimes missing, and at other times attending. Then, suddenly, these juveniles came to our home and threatened us with guns. They busted open into our home and held us and yelled they needed money and knew that I got money from my husband, who was away. I told them I had none. They slapped me and beat my son, and fortunately, my daughter was at her aunt's house and not there. They left us on the floor and told us they were coming back for $150 a week. If we did not pay, they would kill us."

I was shocked. "What did you do, then?"

"Shortly after they left, we decided to pack our bags and run to my sister's house. We talked about it all and decided to leave the country. We did not feel safe anywhere. Too much had happened to us in the town, and we were tired of being afraid."

I could not blame them. Suddenly, the phone rang. "Yes?"

"Ms. Palafox? This is Jerry Hal, prosecutor of the county."

"Oh, hello, Mr. Hal, so glad you returned my call."

"What can I do for you? Your message said it was urgent."

"It is Mr. Hal, and I cannot discuss it over the phone. I have a couple in front of me, clients I am serving right now. Could I see you at your convenience?"

"Sure, how about Monday at 10 am."

"That will be fine, thank you. I will be there."

With that, he hung up, and I turned to my computer and marked my agenda, marked the hour and the day, and then turned to the family again.

"So, you left your town and traveled toward the U.S. border. Where did you go and how did you go?"

Maria began to talk in a matter-of-fact manner. "We left at dawn, with a little money left from what my husband had sent me. We walked, my kids and I, all the way to where we could take a bus to the border between Guatemala and Honduras and managed to cross without any problems. No one stopped us; we simply crossed and continued walking until we could reach Chiapas, where we got help from another Honduran. He had befriended us and said he would help us cross into Mexico. We believed him, so we followed him."

"What a mistake that was," Geovany commented.

I turned to Maria. "How so? He had been a friend?"

Maria shook her head, "He made us believe he was our friend. So, when we followed him across the Mexican border, we did not know where we were going, and he led us to a ranch and told us to stay there, that he was going for food."

"You believed him and went into the ranch?"

"Yes, we thought he would return with food. We were very hungry and thirsty."

"What happened, then?"

Maria shifted her feet and looked down at her shoes. "He lied. Shortly thereafter, four guys walked in with guns and told us we were kidnapped and left some water bottles and some bread, and walked out and locked the door behind them."

"What did you think?"

"I got really scared. Here we had gone through all of this, and now we were kidnapped! I was angry, scared, and did not know how to get us out of this."

I looked at her intently. "But you managed to escape, right?"

She laughed. "It was my daughter, Lisa, in one of their visits with water and bread, one of the guys had put his phone down and gone outside, and she jumped and dialed her father and quickly told him where she thought we were and hung up and put the phone down in its place. When the man returned, he did not know we had used it."

"That was great!" I turned and looked at Lisa, who smiled shyly. It was hard to think this child had the gumption to do what she had done and really saved her family.

Maria continued, "Once Josue knew where we were, because he had not heard from us for days and had been worried sick, he quickly called a family friend and asked him to go down to where we were and help us. But before this happened, Josue got a call from the kidnappers who asked him for $6,000."

"Oh my gosh, that is a lot of money!" I cried out.

Josue replied, "But when it is your family, you do anything to get it, and I did, and I wired it down about the same time that Fernando, my friend, arrived. He arrived and went to the Mexican police and told them about the whole story, and when they arrived at the ranch where my family was, the kidnappers had vanished. They found my family hungry and very thirsty and looking quite sick."

"But he was a sight for sore eyes," Maria chimed in. Both Geovany and Lisa smiled and nodded their heads. "Yeah, we were happy."

"What did the Mexican police do?"

Maria waved her hand in the air, "Oh, nothing much. They took down our names and our story and let us go."

"So, your friend, Fernando, came with you to the U.S. border?"

Maria laughed, "Oh no. He had no intention of doing that. He just took us to a place to clean up and eat, and rest, and then the following day he helped us get to a bus and left us."

I was thinking to myself that at least things had turned for the better. "And the bus brought you to the border?"

"No," Geovany interjected. "We had to get off and find food, and then decided to take the beast as well."

I turned to Maria, "Oh my goodness! You too??"

Maria put her face down and quietly answered, "Yes, we did. We had no choice; we did not have any money."

I could not help but think that the friend had also done them wrong by keeping the money her husband had sent them.

"And how was that ride?"

"It was not bad. We hung on and finally dropped off in Mexico City. Once in the city, we found relatives who could help us house us for a few days and help us reach the border. We were very anxious to reach my husband."

"Now, once you reached the border, you went to the Port of Entry and asked for asylum?"

"Yes," they all answered in unison. I laughed. I took their papers and read where they were held, Hidalgo, Texas. There were no credible fear copies. I turned to Maria.

"Maria, were you or your children ever questioned as to why you were afraid of Honduras and if you feared going back?"

"No, not really. They did not ask much; they were not interested. They just wanted our names and who would come for us. We waited a week until Josue sent the money, and we took the bus to Kentucky."

Silence overtook the office as I wrote on my computer, taking in all the notes of their comments and then making copies of the documents in hand. After a long silence, I turned to them.

"Ok, there are four of you, and it will take me some time to fill out the applications based on what you have told me. I am going to ask you to return next week with two photos of each, passport style, and then we will go over your applications and you will sign them, ok?"

Josue leaned over and asked, "Excuse me, but what will the cost be?"

I leaned back and stared at all of them. I had not even thought of the cost! I really had no idea what to charge them. I realized this would entail a great deal of work and paper since copies had to be made for each case, one for the judge and one for the Chief Counsel. I looked back at them and saw how intently they were looking at me, almost holding their breath.

I turned to Josue, "Just $300."

"That's all?" He was stunned.

I smiled and answered, "Yes, you are asylum seekers, and we do not charge much. I would not have charged at all, but there are four of you and lots of paper involved, and time, and all I am doing is buying you time. I am not a lawyer; I cannot represent you in court."

Josue's eyes glimmered with gratitude. "Thank you, God bless you."

I stood up and reached out my hand to take his outstretched hand. "No problem, glad to do it. It has been a pleasure meeting you."

Maria came up to me and hugged me; I hugged her back. The boys gave me their hands to stretch, and I hugged Lisa as well. "Be safe," I called after them.

Once they had left, Tomas walked into my office. "Another asylum case?"

"Yep, four more, and counting. We have sixty so far and mostly from El Salvador, Honduras, and Guatemala."

"Well, I have a case from Mexico for you on Monday."

"Really? From where in Mexico?"

"From Chiapas, Indian country. A family of six, a couple and four kids."

"Hmm. That will be interesting." I had been sifting papers and stopped and looked at him. "Anything going on?"

Tomas sat down. "Yes, the mother of the kid in Anthony's home called crying. She says she cannot reach him because his phone is blocked, and she is very afraid for him. What can we do?"

I wanted to cuss out but refrained. Then, I turned to Tomas. "Mr. Hal called me when I was consulting with the asylee family, and we have an appointment on Monday. Please, Tomas, call the mother and ask her to get any type of document, something I can take to this guy on Monday. I do not want him to ignore me like he did before."

Tomas stood up. "I will, whatever she has."

That evening, before I went to bed, I again wrote in my diary.

Today's appointment with the Honduran family, Josue, his wife, and children, brought to mind my last experience before I left El Salvador. I had been discussing with an embassy official, who was a friend and a Salvadoran, the differences between the Democrats and the Republicans. She pointed to all the good things that had happened to El Salvador during the Republican administrations, and now, with President Clinton, El Salvador was going to suffer like never before. I had asked why she said that, and she answered, "He is opening the jails of California and sending all the gangs home. When they get here, we will not be able to handle them, and then God help us." And she had been right. When the gangs reached their destination, they were angry to be deported and felt that the country would be theirs. They had been the children who had fled with their parents during the civil war to the United States, seeking shelter. But somehow, once there had gone astray. It was poor parenting or parents working all the time and leaving the children home unattended, who knows? The matter is that some of those children grew up in the streets of major cities of the U.S., like Los Angeles and Chicago, and became the known Salvatrucha or M13. Their family became the gang members, and they were lawless, dangerous, and criminal. When we unleashed them back to their countries of origin, they did not speak Spanish or spoke it badly, and they did not know the country. Therefore, they had no allegiance to it and only thought of themselves. It was self-preservation and the law of the jungle. In El Salvador, they took over street by street, and it reached proportions where people could not cross to *another street without the permission of the opposing gang. The gang members, to survive, began to extort the populace with "protection money". I knew this because I had friends in El Salvador who would complain of the situation, and then I began to get clients, like Josue today, who had suffered because of them. El Salvador, Honduras, and Guatemala, all filled with young, restless criminals seeking to avenge those who crossed them, and becoming a force to reckon with, and one that most governments did not want to oppose. And now their victims are coming here to seek refuge. What goes around comes around."*

Chapter 15

THE APPOINTMENT AT THE PROSECUTORS

When I arrived at City Hall, downtown, I went through security and took the elevator to the fourth floor. Once on the fourth floor, I turned left and walked through the doors of the Prosecutor's office. I walked up to the glassed receptionist window and announced myself.

"Good morning, I am Diana Palafox. I have a meeting with Mr. Hal." I was told to sit down, that he would see me in a few minutes.

It was not long after I had sat down that a young lady opened the door and asked me to follow her inside. We passed by the receptionist's desk and straight on to the back, where Mr. Hal's office stood. He got up and we shook hands.

"So, tell me what I can do for you?" He asked.

"Good morning, Mr. Hal, as you know, I am the director at the Anglo-Latino Center. We service the immigrant community, though the Latino community is the largest, and it has come to my attention that there is a ring of individuals that are kidnapping young girls and boys and are sex trafficking with them."

Everette Hal leaned across the desk. "Do you know who they are?"

"Not specifically, but I have my suspicions. Well, I have the complaint of a mother whose son has been sequestered in a man's home and has been forced to do things against his nature."

"What sorts of things?"

"Sex with other men."

"How old is this child?"

"He is 18 years old. According to the mom, he had arrived from his dad's, who lives in another state, and had not wanted to live with his mother, so he befriended this guy."

"If he did not want to live with his mother, why is she involved, or how does she know that he is a victim?"

I knew he was going to be very critical of what I had to tell him, so I persevered. "He saw himself in a bad way and ran away and called his mother. But before she could drive to where he was to pick him up, this man reached him first and took him back in."

Hal was writing everything down. Then he raised his eyes from his paper and again asked, "Do you know it is a ring, or just this man operating on his own?"

"It is a ring, because other clients have told me that it is common in the Hispanic community to be referred to a number and ask for 'oil change.' If there is an oil change, it means that person can go to whatever place and get what they want. And the site varies. If it were only one person operating the business, it would be one site only, no?"

The prosecutor shook his head. "Not necessarily."

"Mr. Hal, I am here for several reasons. Firstly, if there is a ring preying on our young, I would like to have them busted, and secondly, I would like to have the young man I talked to be freed from the grasp of the person I mentioned."

Everette gazed at me and smiled, "I am sure that is what we would like to do. But I need more information. I need the name of who you think is behind all of this, and where he lives or operates from."

"He is a Panamanian; his name is Anthony Sandoval. He is short, usually has his hair in a bun, and walks with a limp. He is not stocky; he is rather thin. I would say he is about 40 years old but tries to look younger. And he lives near his restaurant."

"Forgive me, Mrs. Palafox, but you sound like you know him well."

"There was a time I did. I was even in his home, visiting who I thought were his kids. The 16-year-old played soccer with my grandson, and we had been invited over after a winning game. It would be months later I found out who he really was and what he delved in, and I became grossed out."

"How so?"

"The 16-year-old, Jorge, was a student at my daughter's school. He had been her student, and later, he confided in her that he did not like living there and that Anthony was not his father. Jorge had come across him on the trains that run through Central America to the United States. Somehow, he was picked up by Anthony and invited to live with him, but he did not want to stay anymore. He let my daughter know that things were not going well."

Everette had continued to jot down some notes. He then put his pen down and stared at the paper. He lifted his eyes to meet mine and told me in a calm manner that there was little he could do. I was shocked. I asked why, and he answered," Mrs. Palafox, we are living in a very political time. My superiors are concerned about our office getting involved in anything dealing with immigrants. Especially helping immigrants."

"Excuse me," I interrupted. "Do you mean that because the victims are immigrants, there is not much your office can do?"

Everette avoided my stare and played with his pen. "It actually is complicated."

I was furious. I stood up and gathered my purse, "Well, Mr. Hal, thank you for seeing me. I hope you have a good day."

With that, I walked out of the office and out into the street and walked quickly and got inside my car. I was shaking. So *that is how it is! If you are an immigrant, you may or may not be here legally, but we do not have time or the inclination to find out anything about a crime done to you. Wow!*

I started the car and drove to the office. When I walked inside, both Tomas and Ines saw me coming in, looking mad. I waved at them to come into my office. When they hurried in, I closed the door.

The Appointment at the Prosecutors

Tomas jumped in, "What happened?"

"Look, we are in a bad way. As immigrants, as far as the police are concerned, we do not amount to anything for them to give us their time to do what is their job to do, look for criminals, arrest them, and throw them in jail."

"But what did he say?" Ines was looking serious.

"He told me it was complicated, that we were living in difficult political times, and that his office could not do anything." I was still bristling from the interview.

Tomas was quiet and then suggested, "Perhaps we can take this to Matt?"

"Oh, Tomas, he is an immigration lawyer..." Then, a thought struck me. "But wait, he can file a lawsuit against his clients in our county. He knows that usually the police never do anything to help our community. And he has been pretty upset about some of our U Visa clients being given the run-around, especially by our county officials."

"Think he might do it?" Tomas asked.

"I don't know," I replied, "but it is worth a try. I will send him an email and see what he thinks."

Tomas got up and walked to the door, "I bet he does. He hates them too."

With that, Tomas and Ines walked out of my office, and I turned to the computer and wrote Matt a long email. I explained who the family was, who Anthony was, and his previous dealings with some kids, my visit with Hall, and my appeal to him.

I did not have to wait long for Matt to answer me. He was just as outraged as I was, and he was willing to file a lawsuit against the county prosecutor's office and others as well. He told me that our county was not the only one. Matter of fact, he was thinking of doing a federal filing. I was thrilled.

The following morning, Tomas ushered in another refugee family, this one from Mexico.

Chapter 16

THE RED TRIANGLE

I was getting used to seeing asylum seekers from many countries in Latin America, but people from Mexico still struck me as odd. As Tomas brought them to my office, I asked them to sit down.

"Good morning," I greeted them. "What can I do for you?" I waved to them to sit down.

The couple sat down, and the man identified himself and his wife. "My name is Mario Ortega Garcia, and this is my wife, Claudia Rendon Rodriguez." They both looked a bit nervous and uneasy.

"Glad to meet you both. Are you here to seek asylum?"

They both nodded. "Yes," replied Mario as he took out some papers from a bag and handed them over to me. I took them and began to read. They were the usual Notice to Appear and other documents. I looked at the middle of the page, and they had entered a month before at El Paso,

TX. It looked like they were within the one-year guideline to submit an asylum application.

"I see here only two Notices to Appear. You came alone, no children?"

Claudia began to sob. Mario tried to pat her hand, and his eyes got moist. "No, no children." He replied hoarsely. "That is one of the reasons we are here. Our children were killed by criminal gangs."

I sat back, trying to take in the profound pain of the moment. I whispered, "I am so sorry." Claudia's large black eyes clouded again with tears, and she could not control her grief. Mario, in his early thirties, a lean, well-built man, leaned to her and put his arm around her to calm her down. But it was hard to calm his wife when he was also in grief and felt the burden of being the stronger of the two to get ahead.

With her head down and in a whisper, Claudia said, "It all started when we were in a hurry to get supplies for our store before it got dark, and we would be in danger from the gangs."

"How so?" I asked.

"I had been after Mario to hurry because we had run out of some foodstuffs and needed to replenish before early the next day."

Mario inserted, "I knew we had to pick up the kids from school, go to the market, get what we needed, and get on the highway before it got late."

With a steady tone, Mario retold in detail what had happened that tragic afternoon. His voice full of emotion wavered as he described the entire scene, going back to 2017.

***

Claudia slid into the passenger seat beside him as they backed onto the highway. The Puebla-Orizaba route, a vital artery for freight traffic, pulsed with movement—trucks and tankers barreling through one of Mexico's busiest corridors. Beneath the surface of the bustling roadways, a web of fuel pipelines crisscrossed the region, linking Puebla to Veracruz, Hidalgo, and the State of Mexico.

Nestled along this expanse, Tecamachalco had long been a town known for its understated beauty—a place where cultural richness, affordability, and a strong sense of community drew tourists and ex-pats alike. For those weary of city clamor, it offered the promise of a quieter life without sacrificing access to the essentials.

But everything changed after 2017.

Claudia and Mario, once confident in the rhythms of their family-run business, had begun to feel the town slipping from their grasp. The creeping influence of the cartels—especially the rise of the New Generation group—brought a wave of violence that shattered the town's sense of safety. Turf wars flared up with chilling frequency, forcing residents to duck for cover as gunfire echoed down the streets. Corpses became a grim fixture—sometimes mutilated, left in bags or worse.

The peace that had once defined Tecamachalco was gone. Where charm once isolated the town in idyllic stillness, it now rendered them vulnerable. Claudia and Mario, like so many others, lived under the shadow of what the region had become: the Red Triangle—a name now synonymous with fear.

There was a certain urgency to their trip to the school. Claudia and Mario had been visited weeks before by men with guns who wanted to extort them. They refused to pay and were threatened. They were given a week to produce the money, or they would suffer consequences.

As they reached the school, Claudia saw her children, and she waved. Their teacher was out on the street waiting with them.

"Hola, hola." Claudia waved. The teacher smiled and waved. The car came to a halt, and both children jumped in. "*Hola mami, hola papy.*" The kids were happy to go home. Juan, the 13-year-old, reached out to his mother, "Mami, can we go to our cousin's? He called me at school. Said his father needed to ask a favor of Papy."

Claudia smiled and turned towards him, "Do you know what he wants?"

Juan shook his head, "Nope, but he was very insistent."

Claudia turned to Mario, "Is it ok, honey, if we stop at Carlo's place?"

Mario was not too happy; he was sensing the afternoon slipping away, and he always got nervous when it got dark. "Ok, but we need to hurry."

With that, he accelerated onto the highway, aiming straight for his brother's house just a few miles away. Another ten miles down stood their food store—fortified with high fences that had become both a shield and a magnet for trouble. The oil thieves didn't just demand protection money; they wanted access to the barn to stash stolen fuel. For Mario, that was a hard no. Allowing it would mean opening the door to rival gangs and drawing government surveillance. He refused to let their livelihood become collateral in someone else's war.

Today, he just wanted to make a quick stop at his brother's, hear what his nephew had to say, then head to the market for produce and return home. Nothing more. Nothing risky.

As they neared his brother's house, he could see his brother and his nephew, Jose, outside waiting for them.

"Hola tio," His nephew greeted him.

"Hola Jose, what is up? What is the urgency?"

Mario's brother, Carlos, came up to the car. "Hola, Mario, hola, Claudia."

He shook hands with them. "Look, hate to ask this, but you know Maria is expecting any minute, and our car is having a few problems. Sometimes it chokes up and needs some time to coax it to start, and it makes me nervous if we must rush to the hospital. Could we switch cars for now, a day or two, and as soon as she goes to the hospital, I will return your car?"

Mario did not want to sound rushed, but he asked, "Look, it is getting dark. We will take your car and go to the market for some stuff, but could Jose take our car and take our kids home? It would not take him long."

Carlos smiled, "Sure, no problem." He seemed relieved.

Mario looked at Claudia. "No problem, right?"

Claudia smiled. "No, none. Just have Jose drive our car home with the kids and come back. We will take yours to the market and home."

They got out of the car and walked over to the area where Carlos had his car and started it. It started without a problem. Before getting in, Claudia went over to the children, gave them a kiss, and waved at Carlos. "Bye, see you later."

"You know," Mario remarked, "The car does seem sluggish. I will look at it when I get home. Right now, we need to rush to the market and get what we need to have the stuff tomorrow when we open our center." Claudia shook her head in acknowledgement. "Yes, we need to hurry."

Just minutes after Jose and the children pulled off the family property and merged onto the highway—heading in the opposite direction—another vehicle crept up behind them. Jose didn't notice it at first. Not until he felt the sudden jolt of metal hitting metal.

The impact snapped his attention to the rearview mirror. "What the hell?!" He shouted, eyes locking on a black sedan with tinted windows. The driver was invisible behind the glare, but something else caught his eye—an arm extending from the passenger side, clutching a gun.

His stomach dropped.

He slammed his foot on the accelerator. The car lunged forward, sending the kids tumbling against their seatbelts.

"Jose! What's going on?" Juan yelled from the back, panic rising in his voice.

"There's a guy pointing a gun at us!" Jose barked, hands gripping the wheel tighter.

Fear thickened in the cabin. He hated speeding—but this wasn't a choice. This was survival. The road curved sharply, and he took it hard, tires screeching. The speedometer climbed past sixty kilometers, then surged toward a hundred. The car trembled under the pressure, but he didn't dare let up.

"Slow down," yelled Juan. "You are scaring us."

"If I slow down, they will kill us." He yelled back. Then the sound of a shot and a bullet grazed the window. Jose swerved and tried to drive zig-zag, but at that speed, he soon lost control, and the car hit a post on the highway and tumbled down the ravine.

***

Claudia's voice drifted through the room like a fading echo, her words blurred by sobs and tears welling in her eyes. It was as if she were speaking from within a fog, recounting—half in grief, half in disbelief—the unthinkable: the loss of her children to the violence of the oil and drug cartels. I leaned forward and handed her a tissue, then quietly placed the box within reach, unsure what else to offer.

Mario sat beside her, unmoving. His expression was carved in stone, unreadable—yet the tension in his jaw betrayed the storm beneath the surface.

"And that is why you left Puebla and made it to the States?" I asked.

Mario shook his head in agreement. "Yes. When we got home that night, my brother Carlos was waiting for us and told us the boys were in the hospital. When we got there, our boys had just passed. Fortunately, Jose lived, but he is paralyzed." His voice got choked up. "We knew then that the week was up, and we had already paid the consequences, but there would be more if we didn't give them money."

I was appalled. "But couldn't you go to the police and file a complaint?"

Mario smirked. "The police? For what? We never know if they are part of the gang or too scared to do anything." Again, he shook his head, "No, they are no good. No one can protect you. You must give in, or you will be killed."

I felt awful, sad, and aghast that this sort of thing was happening all over Mexico.

"We barely had time to grieve our kids and bury them. All we had was the store, so we closed it up. We really had nothing now and felt it was best to leave before we were killed."

I had finished writing the last paragraph of the asylum application. I got up and walked over to them and reached out to them. I gave Claudia a hug and shook Mario's hand. "I am so sorry for your loss."

Then I walked back to my chair and sat down. "I will finish writing more of the details. As soon as I do, I will mail your application to the court. I checked; your MASTER hearing will be in November of this year. "

Mario cleared his throat and regained composure. "Will we need a lawyer?"

I nodded. "Normally, for the Master hearing, we do not ask our clients to take a lawyer. But now, with this new administration that hates immigrants, you are better off going with a lawyer. Just in case. The unthinkable happens often."

Claudia nodded as she finished drying her eyes and began to regain composure.

I rose and shook her hand. "That will be all for now."

Mario startled and said," Aren't you going to charge us?"

His comment brought me back to earth. In this moment of sensibility, I had not wanted to talk about money. "No, I don't think…"

He interrupted, "No, I insist. Please tell us how much we owe you?"

I stared at them both and shook my head. "All right, just $300."

"Are you sure that is all?" Claudia asked in disbelief.

I nodded in agreement. "Yes, that is enough."

Mario opened his wallet. Claudia took his hand and then said, "Give her $500."

Mario agreed, and with that, he gave me crisp five-hundred-dollar bills.

I thanked them both, gave them their receipt, and then walked them to the door. "Please let me know as soon as you receive the stamped page from the court."

They thanked me, blessed me, and walked out.

When I got home, I was very weary and haunted. It was as if the weight of all those years was starting to take a toll on me. I had started working with the immigrant population in 2001, and here we were, in 2025, and not much had changed. All those years of helping and suffering with them. Seeing how politics changed, but nothing changed for them. It was as if time were static for them. There was no way out. No one wanted to really deal with the immigration problem. Everyone felt it was a problem, both Democrats and Republicans, but no one moved the needle. There was the exception of President Reagan in 1985, who enabled over three million to legalize, and then President Obama, who was forced to do something and issued an Executive Order to bring about the Deferred Action for Childhood Arrivals, the DACA kids. But other than that, there was no major legislation, no major Immigration reform. Everyone admitted that the system was dysfunctional, that it needed to be reformed, but no one was willing to make changes. It simply kept getting worse and worse.

The first Trump Administration practically dismantled immigration law. The last thing they wanted was to help immigrants. If anything, President Trump had been elected because of his hard and cruel stance on immigration.

And now, in the second MAGA administration, things were worse, more cruel, harder to accept. Immigrants were no longer human beings; they were being treated as animals, all criminals. As masked ICE agents or would-be agents corralled and drag people from their work or out of their cars, or on the street, it was obvious that fear was to be the order of the day. Hopefully, if immigrants feared their lives so much, it would propel them to leave the country. That was the whole point: to make life fearful and miserable and unbearable. Not much different than their home country.

According to "The American Immigration Council's Report: Mass Deportations," there are approximately 13 million undocumented immigrants in the U.S. It is totally unrealistic to think that they would all be deported quickly. Right now, our present institutional capacity in all jails and all prisons is for 1.9 million people. Detention camps would have to be built, and we are already seeing that happen. Also, there is a need for 1000 courtrooms, more lawyers, and security personnel. With the new "Beautiful Bill," ICE has just been promised millions of dollars to enlarge its force.

The report also points out that there is a backlog of 3.6 million cases in our immigration courts. Who would have priority, the ones already in line or the recently detained? We are already seeing people being held in jails, and they will have to wait for the backlog to subside. And again, we are talking about keeping people in jail for a long time before being removed. Again, more cost.

Mass deportations will cause labor shortages in construction, agriculture, and the hospitality sector. If construction companies are affected, the price of housing is going to go up. In agriculture, the undocumented workers are by far the most working in the fields, picking fruit and vegetables from Florida, California, Texas, and Washington. Grocery prices are going to go through the roof. In the hospitality sector, there are hotels, people who do housecleaning, maintenance, and food preparers. Prices all around are going to increase significantly.

As industries suffer, every American taxpayer will be impacted by the fiscal burden of mass deportations, and it will be exacerbated by the reduced tax base that it will create.

Something that is never said is how much undocumented workers pay in federal, state, and local taxes. According to the report, they paid $46.8 billion in federal taxes and $29.3 billion in state and local taxes. They also contributed, but will never see a benefit, $22.6 billion to Social Security and $5.7 billion to Medicare.

Deep down inside, I knew I did not have the stomach for all of this anymore. I was getting older and tired. I had to prepare and train my young team to resist, protest, and take on the mantle. I knew that Tomas was up to the task and then some. He had grown into a highly respected and well-liked Accredited Representative. He and our team were as committed to the people as I was and ready to take over. Our last hire, a remarkable American young woman, Stacey Williams, spoke Spanish fluently and had a charismatic touch with clients. It didn't take long for her to obtain her accreditation so she could help with the load of asylees that kept coming. The team was ready to fight on.

With that last thought in mind, I decided to turn to my diary. I wanted to put down my ideas before I forgot them. I was tired and needed to sleep, but this was more important; I didn't want to forget my thoughts, so I began writing:

It never amazes me how many clients always bless me and wish me many blessings for me and my family. I know they are grateful, but it is only my job. This is what I am meant to do. More often than not, I am appalled at the horrendous stories, the suffering, and the almost unending cycle of violence. Regardless of people's loss, either of their lives or property, our law does not consider any of it with merit to offer them asylum. According to Human Rights First, since 2018, the Justice Department has eliminated domestic and gang violence as grounds for asylum. Since that decision, the rate of asylum approvals for women from Central America has plummeted. To win an asylum case is very difficult. Even if there is a "credible fear" factor in the case. And with the new MAGA administration, it will be even more difficult. The circumstances and situations in many countries, like Mexico, are dire. In Mexico, for instance, aside from drugs, cartels now also deal with gasoline theft, and Puebla has become a strategic state for the illegal fuel industry.[7]

It angers me that in 2018, Immigration Judges considered that cartel persecution or problems with criminal gangs did not qualify for asylum. Like in the case of Saul Ramirez, how many have escaped from these vicious hands and come to seek solace and peace, only to be denied asylum and turned back? It does not make sense.

Today, 13 million undocumented men, women, and children live in legal limbo—working, studying, and raising families in a country that refuses to recognize them. The legacy of the

---

[7] "The Red Triangle is a lucrative zone for oil smugglers and a major battleground for the control of the oil theft business. In addition, violence has increased in recent years because Puebla is one of the states with the least resources invested in the fight against organized crime. While there are states that allocate between 5 and 6 percent of their year budget to this initiative, Puebla barely had a 2 percent spend in 2019; more than half of Puebla's total spend is used to cover outstanding fees from previous years. Puebla was one of the most peaceful states in Mexico prior to the arrival of the Jalisco New Generation Cartel (CJNG) in early 2017." (**Source:** La Jornada; Lantia Intelligence; Borderland Beat archives pg.112)

Trump-era "Zero Tolerance" policy still echoes: over 5,000 children were separated from their parents at the border, many without a system to reunite them. Deportations surged, and fear seeped into every corner of immigrant life. In 2025, ICE raids and family detentions continue under hardline policies, often in brutal form, without following the law: No warrants, not caring if those detained are legal or citizens, leaving families still too afraid to go to work, report crimes, or seek medical care. This administration is implementing concentration camps, a la **Alligator Alcatraz,** as an example of cruelty and sheer inhumane management of human beings.

But history reminds us, and I want to believe, that progress is possible. The **1965 Immigration and Nationality Act** dismantled racist national-origin quotas and opened the door to a more diverse America. In 1986, the **Immigration Reform and Control Act (IRCA)** granted legal status to nearly 3 million undocumented immigrants—proof that Congress can act with courage and compassion.

Today's problem is not just policy—it's paralysis. MAGA-era enforcement has deepened the divide between "us" and "them," criminalizing neighbors and tearing apart communities. The human cost is staggering, and the moral cost even more so.

We need a path forward. A bipartisan bill could offer legal status to **DREAMers**, streamline the **farm-worker visa** system, and fund the **USCIS backlog** that keeps families waiting in limbo. Dust off the bill President Biden sent to Congress, an offer to apply for a work permit with proof of presence in 2021. Then, after five years, if there are no criminal records in their background, they can apply for legal residence. But legislation alone won't move the needle—grassroots power will. That means phone banks, town halls, and letter-writing campaigns in every district. It means reminding lawmakers that immigration is not a wedge issue—it's a human one.

The cold sweep of "Zero Tolerance" may have chilled the national conscience, but it hasn't frozen our resolve. We just need to remember who we are and what we stand for.

Still, I remain steadfast. History's arc may bend slowly, but it cannot be permanently diverted. One day, the voices of everyday people will rise with enough force to bring about the recognition so long overdue—that immigrants are the lifeblood of this nation. We are the fabric and the embroidery. We thread new patterns and designs into the American tapestry, making it vibrant, unique, and extraordinary. We are the sum of all humanity.

I closed the computer, turned off the light, and crawled into bed. It wasn't long before sleep overtook me.

Acknowledgments

This book would not exist without the countless immigrants who shared their stories with honesty and vulnerability. Your resilience inspired every page.

To the priest who first opened the door to this journey—thank you for seeing something in me I hadn't yet seen in myself.

To my colleagues in the Hispanic Ministry and the Center, your tireless work and unwavering belief in justice made real change possible.

To the lawyer from Louisville who has been a mentor to me and a friend, seeing that I stayed on the right lane.

To my publishing consultant and her editorial staff, thank you for your patience and perfect guidance.

To my friends and family who listened, challenged, and supported me, even when the road was hard—your love gave me strength.

And to every reader willing to walk alongside these stories: may you be moved, may you be changed, and may you never again see immigration as a problem, but as a promise.

To Faby, thank you for your gift of friendship and caring.
You are a talented artist with a great heart.

www.ingramcontent.com/pod-product-compliance
Lightning Source LLC
LaVergne TN
LVHW041659060526
838201LV00043B/487